American Crossroad of Trust

Thomas H. Fairbanks
A Believing Patriot

Printed by CreateSpace, An Amazon.com Company

ISBN: 1983636398
ISBN-13: 978-1983636394

DEDICATION

This is dedicated to the wisdom and memory of our Founding Fathers; and to the spirit and fortitude of all true patriots, *"who more than self their country loved, and mercy more than life"* and are willing to stand for truth, right, family, peace, and freedom. *"America! America! May God thy [souls] refine, till all success be nobleness, and every gain divine,"* (*American the Beautiful*, Katharine Lee Bates, 1910)

John & Judy:

Nothing is as it appears and
we stand at the crossroad of trust.

" Believe "

CONTENTS

ACKNOWLEDGMENTS

The information provided here is a compilation from a wide variety of sources, along with the author's personal and professional experiences. Direct quotes are noted as such, while other references and information has been edited for ease of understanding. We wish to thank those who have contributed, both knowingly and unknowingly to this work.

FAIR USE NOTICE: The copyrighted material contained herein, the use of which has not always been specifically authorized by the copyright owner, is provided in an effort to advance understanding of political, economic, and educational issues. There has been no attempt to infringe or compete with any copyrights in this publication and it is believed that this constitutes a 'fair use' of any such copyrighted material as provided for in section 107 of the US Copyright Law. For more information go to: http://www.law.cornell.edu/uscode/17/107.shtml.

Cover by:
David Fairbanks
BeholderGames.Com
Brigham City, Utah

American Crossroad of Trust

The founders of our country revealed this nation's source of *"strength"* when declaring our independence from the tyranny of England's rule: *"We hold these truths to be self-evident, that all men are created equal, that they are endowed by their Creator with certain unalienable Rights, that among these are Life, Liberty and the pursuit of Happiness,"* These fundamental beliefs have been tested throughout our continuous growth as a nation and have been continually challenged to see if we would keep them above mankind and his manipulations.

The blessings and benefits of the freedom that we enjoy here in America have allowed us, as a nation, to raise a generation in relative peace. As an explanation, columnist Leonard Pitts Jr. reported the following just after the attack on the Twin Towers on September 11, 2001:

"Let me tell you about my people. We are a vast and quarrelsome family; a family rent by racial, cultural, political and class division, but a family nonetheless. We're frivolous, yes, capable of expending tremendous emotional energy on pop cultural minutiae, a singer's revealing dress, a ball team's misfortune, a cartoon mouse.

"We're wealthy; too, spoiled by the ready availability of trinkets and material goods, and maybe because of that, we walk through life with a certain sense of blithe entitlement. We are

1

fundamentally decent, though — peace-loving and compassionate. We struggle to know the right thing and to do it. And we are, the overwhelming majority of us, people of faith, believers in a just and loving God.

"Some people — you, perhaps — think that any or all of this makes us weak. You're mistaken. We are not weak. Indeed, we are strong in ways that cannot be measured by arsenals."

For many of us, we have felt that the United States of America is the greatest nation on the face of the earth. We have never been the aggressor, but always a defender of those who seek liberty over tyranny. Our belief in freedom and the rights of others to choose often restrained us in the time of decision, and as a nation we tended to wait before we acted. We have believed that ours was the only nation that has been victorious in war and never claimed any territory as a prize of conquest. Showing to the world our brotherhood, after coming off conqueror, by pouring literally billions to revive those who have been our enemies. From our abundance we have given billions in aid to assist the poor throughout the world and have never asked for anything in return. Showing by example that our compassionate actions are nothing more than an expression of our belief that all men are entitled to *Life, Liberty and the Pursuit of Happiness.*

As a nation, our sense of security was shattered on September 11, 2001 by the seemingly unprovoked and senseless act of man's inhumanity to man, in a magnitude never before witnessed on United States soil. And our naive assumption that our might and abundances would protect us began to topple with the collapse of the Twin Towers in New York City.

America was in peril and the atrocities, which have followed, were a intentional attack on the fundamental trust that holds our civilization together. It was an assault on people and on the solvency of an economic structure, and it was a disruption of the stability, freedom and protection a global community of trading nations provides. But in the wake of the destruction, it was our leaders, who had been entrusted to protect and serve, and

American Business, sensing the benefit of a seemingly greater enemy, who took the opportunity to reveal the dubious business practices of Enron, WorldCom, Tyco, and others, with confessions that they had been duplicitous in their duties.

And our biggest casualty in all these events was *trust*, the trust of our people, their trust in their personal safety and the country's security, along with their trust in our leaders and the economy. Some would like us to believe that our real struggle is between rich and poor, or East and West or even between the primacy of a religion's teachings. But it isn't about rich and poor. It isn't about East and West and it isn't one religion versus another. It's about stability, freedom and protection for everyone — it's about trust.

There remain many who are confused and scrutinizing our response to these events while looking for a collective weakness. Collective because as nations, individuals and businesses we're bound together by a vast web of treaties, laws and rules of engagement. Though sometimes complex and inefficient, these rules have prevented us from devolving and dropping into complete chaos, they support our civilization and our very existence.

These atrocities became a stark wake-up call that there are many who have been raised to hate us, and all that this county stands for, and we have been further reminded in the aftermath of the chain reaction of wannabe-copycats seeking their moment of fame and savvy political activists who perpetuate divides in the name of a greater good, economic turmoil, and even the housing crisis of 2008, that inhumanity knows no borders.

Now that we have joined in the turmoil and confusion, our concerns about the condition of our society and the destructive motives of others need to be examined. It is clearly evident that those responsible for these attacks, wanted us to stop trusting each other, our intuitions and ourselves. (And you can believe this with certainty - those who would perpetrate disloyal acts will seek to do them again.) Yet it was our leaders and American Business, some protected by political influence, that had accomplished what the "alleged terrorists" had only hoped to do.

Even in our court system here in America, we have always championed the importance and our expectation of a level playing field. During Supreme Court Justice Elena Kagan's confirmation hearing in 2010, she described the courts as "level playing fields" where citizens receive "equal justice." This ideal is engraved in marble on the front of the Supreme Court building: "Equal Justice Under Law." Regrettably, as a result of the blurring of the boundaries of conduct, no longer are we, the people confident that the rules of the game can even be recognized, let alone that they will be followed. Time once was when we knew our ethical limits and what could be expected. But as 'greed became good,' our traditional values seemingly fell by the wayside, leaving in its wake the destruction of trust.

Truth and trust are the essential elements that bind us together and enable us to move forward in a single, united front. Everything we do must build and underscore trust. Trust that we can deal justly with each other. Trust that we can make airline travel safer and more secure without reducing civil liberties or expectations of privacy. Trust that we can go forward enabling electronic commerce with no risk that personal data will be misused. Trust that we can empower law enforcement to better track and arrest criminals without fear that civil liberties will be constrained. Trust that agreements among ourselves and with other nations will empower, not inhibit their citizens. And trust that we will keep our word.

Our Founding Fathers gave grave warning about our future if we failed to obey and observe the principles of our Constitution: "*One of the greatest American historians of the last generation was John Fiske. He caught the spirit of the Founders and studied their writings. He also saw some dangerous trends away from the Founders' basic formula of sound government. He therefore wrote a prophecy which Americans of our own day might ponder with profit: "If the day should ever arrive (which God forbid!) when the people of the different parts of our country shall allow their local affairs to be administered by prefects sent from Washington, and when the self government of the states shall have been so far lost as that of the departments of France, or even so closely limited as that of the counties of England -- on that day the political career of the American people will have been robbed of its most interesting and valuable features, and the usefulness of this nation will be lamentably impaired,"* (W. Cleon Skousen, "The Five Thousand Year Leap" 1981, pg. 240)

"In May 1805, while serving as President, Jefferson wrote to Dr. George Logan. He was concerned with elements of extremism pushing toward the extreme right which, to the Founders, meant 'anarchy,' He wrote: "I see with infinite pain the bloody schism which has taken place among our friends in Pennsylvania and New York, and will probably take place in other States. The main body of both sections mean well, but their good intentions will produce great public evil,) Like President Washington, Jefferson saw the need for maintaining the government in the balanced center where the Constitution had placed it. He wrote to Governor George Clinton in 1803, 'Our business is to march straight forward ... without either turning to the right or left.' With both of the eagle's wings flying -- one solving problems, the other preserving resources and freedom -- the American future could not help but ascend to unprecedented heights of wealth and influence," (W. Cleon Skousen, "The Five Thousand Year Leap" 1981, pg. 28-29)

"Peering down through the corridor of time, Franklin proclaimed his prophetic judgment as to what could be expected if future generations of Americans permitted the lure of high salaries to be associated with public offices. Here are the remarkably profound insights from the "Sage of Philadelphia" to the members of the Constitutional Convention: 'Sir, though we may set out in the beginning with moderate salaries, we shall find that such will not be of long continuance. Reasons will never be wanting for proposed augmentations; and there will always be a party for giving more to the rulers, that the rulers may be able in return to give more to them. Hence, as all history informs us, there has been in every state and kingdom a constant kind of warfare between the governing and the governed, the one striving to obtain more for its support, and the other to pay less. And this has alone occasioned

great convulsions, actual civil wars, ending either in dethroning of the princes or enslaving of the people. Generally, indeed, the ruling power carries its point, and we see the revenues of princes constantly increasing, and we see that they are never satisfied, but always in want of more. The more the people are discontented with the oppression of taxes, the greater need the prince has of money to distribute among his partisans, and pay the troops that are to suppress all resistance, and enable him to plunder at pleasure." (W. Cleon Skousen, "The Five Thousand Year Leap" 1981, pg. 67-68)

"Since the genius of the American system is maintaining the eagle in the balanced center of the spectrum, the Founders warned against a number of temptations which might lure subsequent generations to abandon their freedoms and their rights by subjecting themselves to a strong federal administration operating on the collectivist Left. They warned against the "welfare state" where the government endeavors to take care of everyone from the cradle to the grave. Jefferson wrote: 'If we can prevent the government from wasting the labors of the people, under the pretense of taking care of them, they must become happy.' They warned against confiscatory taxation and deficit spending. Jefferson said it was immoral for one generation to pass on the results of its extravagance in the form of debts to the next generation. He wrote: '... we shall all consider ourselves unauthorized to saddle posterity with our debts, and morally bound to pay them ourselves; and consequently within what may be deemed the period of a generation, or the life [expectancy] of the majority.' Every generation of Americans struggled to pay off the national debt up until the present one. The Founders also warned that the only way for the nation to prosper was to have equal protection of 'rights,' and not allow the government to get involved in trying to provide equal distribution of 'things.' They also warned against the pooling of property as advocated by the proponents of communism. Samuel Adams said they had done everything possible to make the ideas of socialism and communism unconstitutional. Said he: 'The Utopian schemes of leveling [re-distribution of the wealth and a community of goods [central ownership of the means of production and distribution], are as visionary and impractical

as those which vest all property in the Crown. [These ideas] are arbitrary, despotic, and, in our government, unconstitutional." (W. Cleon Skousen, "The Five Thousand Year Leap" 1981, pg. 29-30)

Historically, as a people we have fled oppressive government and tyranny. It was the driving motivation for immigration to the New World and the constant westward movement in search of the freedom to become what we want to be.

Sadly, almost half the population has been seduced into believing that government is the answer to all our social and economic problems instead of a catalyst to their resolution. Unfortunately, we find ourselves, again, in contradiction to the warnings of our Founding Fathers, which has resulted in U.S. Government involvement and regulations that have stifled job creation, growth, and the expansion of small businesses which is the heart of the economy, and set us up to be the world's unwitting police force.

Thomas H. Fairbanks

World War II - The Other Side of the Story
As told by Robert B. Stinnett

In the preface of his book titled, *Day of Deceit: The Truth about FDR and Pearl Harbor* (New York, Free Press, 2000) Robert B. Stinnett writes, "My sole purpose is to uncover the true story of events leading up to the devastating attack on the naval base [at Pearl Harbor] and adjoining Army facilities, and to document that it was not a surprise to President Franklin Delano Roosevelt and many of his top military and policy advisors.... Roosevelt believed that his countrymen would rally only to oppose an overt act of war on the United States. The decision he made, in concert with his advisors, was to provoke Japan through a series of actions into an overt act: the Pearl Harbor attack. As I have discovered in the course of seventeen years of archival research and personal interviews with US Navy cryptographers, the answer to Roosevelt's dilemma is found in an extraordinary number of documents whose release I have been able to obtain through Freedom of Information Act requests. These papers outline deliberate steps that were planned and implemented to elicit the overt action that catapulted America into the war, and devastated military forces at Pearl Harbor and other Pacific bases. Eight steps were suggested to provoke a Japanese attack. Shortly after reviewing these, Roosevelt put them into effect. After the eight provocations had been taken, Japan responded. On November 27 and 28, 1941, US military commanders were given this order: 'The United States desires that Japan commit the first overt act.' According to Secretary of War Henry L. Stimson, the order came directly from President Roosevelt.... Not only did we undertake provocative steps, we intercepted and decoded military cables. We knew the attack was coming.... The commanders in Hawaii,

Admiral Husband Kimmel and Lieutenant General Walter Short, were deprived of intelligence that might have made them more alert to the risks entailed in Roosevelt's policy, but they obeyed his direct order: 'The United States desires that Japan commit the first overt act.' More than 200,000 documents and interviews have led me to these conclusions. I am indebted to the Freedom of Information Act and its author, the late Congressman John Moss (D, CA) for making it possible for me to tell this story,) [xiii-xiv]

"Stinnett conclusively demonstrates with vast and incontrovertible documentary evidence that in order to precipitate an unwilling American public into supporting intervention in the Second World War, President Roosevelt oversaw the contrivance and deployment of a closely-guarded secret plot to goad the Japanese into attacking Pearl Harbor. The plan was set in motion in October 1940, and its development closely monitored through decoded intercepts of Japanese diplomatic and military radio communications. Knowledge of the plan was limited to 13 Roosevelt administration members and chief military officers, and 21 members of Naval Intelligence and related operations. Once it produced the intended result and the attack impended, the Pacific fleet's modern naval vessels were sent to sea from Pearl Harbor, leaving seven antiquated World War One battleships as decoys. Meanwhile, the Japanese fleet was tracked with radio intercepts from its formation off the Kuril Islands on November 16, and its sailing for Hawaii on November 26; its course was cleared of all shipping with a Vacant Sea order on the 22nd; and Pearl Harbor naval patrols were ordered out of the area on the 25th. Intelligence of the impending attack was withheld from the officers (Admiral Kimmel and General Short) charged with defending Pearl Harbor, who were kept uninformed of the plan and intelligence of the impending attack, and scape-goated afterward. A coverup of the entire operation was maintained through eight official and Congressional investigations between 1941 and 1946, and down to Strom Thurmond's inquiry in 1995. Stinnett's forty-seven pages of Appendices (p. 261-308) present photographic reproductions of essential documents obtained from Federal archives through the Freedom of Information Act, as well as numerous other documents reproduced in the body of the text, and 65 pages (p. 309-374) of closely detailed and referenced notes, all of which copiously and conclusively document Stinnett's factual assertions, arguments and conclusions. His voluminous research files and notes are deposited at the Hoover Institute library at Stanford.

"It is notable that Lt. Commander McCollum's 'eight-action memo' for inciting war with the Japanese is dated October 7, 1940; that its sixth action was set in motion on October 8, its first, second and seventh on October 16; and that, campaigning for a third term as president in Boston on October 30, FDR said: 'I have said this before, but I shall say it again and again and again: Your boys are not going to be sent into any foreign wars;' on November 1 in Brooklyn he said 'I am fighting to keep our people out of foreign wars. And I will keep on fighting;' at Rochester on the 2nd he said 'Your national government ... is equally a government of peace — a government that intends to retain peace for the American people;' the same day in Buffalo he asserted 'Your President says this country is not going to war;' and in Cleveland on the 3rd he declared 'The first purpose of our foreign policy is to keep our country out of war.' These quotations are from William Henry Chamberlin, 'How Franklin Roosevelt Lied America Into War,' in Harry Elmer Barnes, Perpetual War for Perpetual Peace (Caldwell, Idaho, Caxton, 1953,) Chapter Eight, p. 485-491.

"Previous accounts have claimed that the United States had not cracked Japanese military codes prior to the attack. We now know this is wrong. Previous accounts have insisted that the Japanese fleet maintained strict radio silent. This, too, is wrong. The truth is clear: FDR knew,) [5]

"'A memorandum circulated in Washington, originating in the Office of Naval Intelligence (ONI) and addressed to two of FDR's most trusted advisors suggests ... provoking Japan into an overt act of war against the United States. It was written by Lieutenant Commander Arthur H. McCollum, head of the Far East desk of the ONI.' [6] Stinnett does not address the obvious conclusion that McCollum was instructed to design such a plan; it is highly improbable that this key policy was initiated by a junior officer on his own initiative. McCollum's memo is photographically reproduced in Appendix A, 261-267]

"Lieutenant Commander McCollum's five-page 'eight-action memo, dated October 7, 1940 ... puts forward ... a plan intended to engineer a situation that would mobilize reluctant America into joining Britain's struggle against the German armed forces.... Its eight actions call for virtually inciting a Japanese attack on American ground, air, and naval forces in Hawaii, as well as on British and Danish colonial outposts in the Pacific region.... McCollum oversaw the routing of communications intelligence to FDR from early 1940 to December 7, 1941 and provided the President with intelligence reports on Japanese military and diplomatic strategy. Every intercepted and decoded Japanese military and diplomatic report destined for the White House went through the Far East Asia section of ONI, which he oversaw. The section served as a clearinghouse for all categories of intelligence reports.... Each report prepared by McCollum for the President was based on radio intercepts gathered and decoded by a worldwide network of American military cryptographers and radio intercept operators.... Few people in America's government or military knew as much about Japan's activities and intentions as McCollum.' [8]

"Appendix E 307-308 lists the 34 'Americans who were cleared for unrestricted access to decoded and translated Japanese diplomatic intercepts.' They comprise FDR, his Secretaries of War, State and the Navy (Stimson, Hull, Knox,) three senior military staff members (Gen. Marshall, Adm. Stark, Rear Adm. Ingersoll) and three key naval staff officers, two field commanders (Gen. MacArthur, Adm. Hart,) FDR's naval aide (Capt. Beardall) who acted as his liaison with ONI, and 21 senior officers and cryptographers of ONI and other intelligence operations. Kimmel and Short were pointedly restricted in their access.

"McCollum's memorandum lists eight actions that he predicted would provoke a Japanese attack:

A. Make an arrangement with Britain for use of British bases in the Pacific, particularly Singapore.

B. Make an arrangement with Holland for the use of base

facilities and acquisition of supplies in the Dutch East Indies [now Indonesia].

C. Give all possible aid to the Chinese government of Chiang Kai-shek.

D. Send a division of long-range heavy cruisers to the Orient, Philippines, or Singapore.

"E. Send two divisions of submarines to the Orient.

F. Keep the main strength of the US Fleet, now in the Pacific, in the vicinity of the Hawaiian islands.

G. Insist that the Dutch refuse to grant Japanese demands for undue economic concessions, particularly oil.

H. Complete embargo all trade with Japan, in collaboration with a similar embargo imposed by the British Empire,) [8. Stinnett shows the routing of this memo to senior ONI officers and thence to Sect. of the Navy Knox and to FDR 8-9.]

"Action C was already US policy. Action F was initiated on October 8, 1940; Actions A, B, and G by October 16, 1940; D and E by November 12, 1940. The plan was completed on July 26, 1941 with Action H. [Chap. 1 n. 8 p. 311-312; 120 ff. & passim]

"Admiral Richardson, commander of the Pacific Fleet, opposed FDR's orders to station the fleet at Pearl Harbor as putting the fleet at risk, so FDR replaced him with Kimmel and placed Admiral Anderson of ONI as Kimmel's third in command at Pearl Harbor, to supervise the radio intercept operation there unbeknownst to Kimmel. [10-14; 33-34] 'Anderson was sent to Hawaii as an intelligence gatekeeper.' [36] When he arrived he established his personal housing well away from "Pearl Harbor, out of range of the coming attack. Though he was commander of the seven battleships which bore the brunt of the attack with the loss of well over a thousand lives, Adm. Anderson was safe at home on the other side of the mountain when the attack came. [36-37; 244, 247]

"In early January 1941, the Japanese decided that in the event of hostilities with the US they would commence with a surprise attack on Pearl Harbor. American intelligence learned of this plan on January 27. [30-32]

"Among the radio intercepts was a bomb plot map of Pearl Harbor developed by a Japanese spy at their consulate in Honolulu to aid in targeting. This, too, was kept from Kimmel and Short. The ONI operatives tracking this spy's operations kept the FBI and other counter-intelligence operations away from him in order to sequester this — and all — intelligence. [66 etc.; 83-97, 98-110]

"Roosevelt discovered Germany's plans for the invasion of Russian through a [Japanese diplomatic] Purple [code] intercept on June 14, 1941,) [69. He informed Churchill immediately, or Churchill learned from shared intelligence. Churchill quotes his cable to FDR referring to it dated June 15 in his memoir, The Second World War, vol. 3]

"Radio intercepts revealed the formation of the Japanese fleet near the Kuril Islands north of Japan beginning November 16, 1941 and tracked it across the Pacific to Hawaii from November 26 through the first week of December. [41-59 etc.]

"On 22 November 1941, a week after the Japanese fleet began to assemble and four days before it set off for Hawaii, Adm. Ingersoll issued a "Vacant Sea" order that cleared the path of the Japanese fleet of all shipping, and on 25 November ordered Kimmel to withdraw his ships patrolling the area from which the aerial attack would be staged. [144-145]

"Shortly before the Japanese attack, Chief of Naval Operations Admiral Stark (one of the 34 Americans in on the plot) ordered Kimmel to dispatch his aircraft carriers with a large escort to deliver planes to Wake and Midway Islands. 'On orders from Washington, Kimmel left his oldest vessels inside Pearl Harbor and sent twenty-one modern warships, including his two aircraft carriers, west toward Wake and Midway... With their departure the warships remaining in Pearl Harbor were mostly 27-year-old relics of World War I.' That is, the battleships sunk at Pearl Harbor and their crews were used as decoys. [152-154]

"FDR kept close tabs on the plot's final unfolding. [161-176]

"Pearl Harbor's Battleship Row and its old dilapidated warships presented a mouth-watering target. But it was a major strategic mistake for the Empire. Japan's 360 warplanes should have concentrated on Pearl Harbor's massive oil stores ... and destroyed the industrial capacity of the Navy's dry docks, machine shops, and repair facilities.... By the Battle of Midway in June 1942, America had regained the offensive; repaired US warships staged from the relatively undamaged Pearl Harbor naval base [as well as the modern fleet absent during the attack], sank four of the aircraft carriers that had attacked them six months before,) [249] At the Battles of Midway and Coral Sea, a month earlier, the US Navy permanently destroyed the offensive capacity of the Japanese Navy in the eastern Pacific, and permanently crippled its defensive capacity in the western Pacific. [George N. Crocker, Roosevelt's Road To Russia (Chicago, Regnery, 1959) 166] Thus there was no possibility thereafter of a Japanese attack or invasion of the West Coast, and this was known several months before the internment of West Coast Japanese American citizens commenced in August 1942.

"The coverup of the operation commenced immediately afterward, continued through eight Congressional investigations during and just after the war, with the purging and withholding of documents and false testimony by participants and others [253-260 & passim; 309-310], and persisted through the Congressional hearings chaired by Strom Thurmond in 1995 [257-258]. At the date of publication (2000) numerous documents were still withheld from Stinnett or released in extensively censored form, and the pretense that the Japanese naval codes had not been deciphered and that the Japanese fleet maintained radio silence was still being maintained."

[The foregoing information was obtained from the following internet sources deemed to be reliable:

15

www.lewrockwell.com/2016/12/no_author/pearl-harbor-fake-news-story/

http://www.washingtonsblog.com/2016/12/pearl-harbor-facts-proof.html#more-63816]

This is a far different view of America's patriotism, and our involvement in world affairs, than the carefully crafted image I was proudly raised to believe in, and it speaks volumes about us never having been the aggressor.

Kingship - Our Model of Business

Let's take a look at the typical business model of American business. It is a top-down approach based on a pyramid, an organizational style that emphasizes the vision and directives of upper management, which flows down from the top to the subordinates below. This approach is based upon a firm foundation, representative of the strength and longevity of the ancient Egyptian pyramids, and is believed to unify a company behind ones' purpose, direction, and standard, that is dictated from above and spread throughout the entire organization.

Some suggest that this approach allows a business to reliably give customers the same quality experience with standardized offerings, which can be rolled out on a grand scale, more cheaply than non-standardized products and services. The organizational structure dictates how the work is divided and with its unity of command, this approach, allows an organization to avoid confusion in times of crisis, with clear lines of authority, because the top-down approach demands obedience.

The detriment associated with this business model lies in the voluminous historical evidence that shows when most individuals gain a little authority, as they suppose, they will immediately begin to exercise compulsion or control over those underneath their rule.

The focus is naturally at the top of the pyramid, which brings with it attention, recognition and all kinds of accolades and perks to the individual in charge, the Chief Executive Officer or Head Honcho, who unfortunately in many organizations is crowned as the King. Underneath the King are the Nobles, the privileged class, who support and advise the King, and who also become the recipients of indulgent practices known as nepotism, cronyism and favoritism, which allows the Nobles to be ingratiated with preferential treatment reserved for relatives, friends and ardent supporters of the King. Under the Nobles are the Knights, the enforcers, whose job it is to carry out the dictates of the King. At the bottom are the Peasants, the workers and those indentured to do the King's bidding, who are known by the special title they hold as, PEONS because everything rolls down hill.

This system actually has a rigid structure of its classes and except for the illusion of manifest destiny, those who are born commoners can expect to die as commoners. There are no real provisions for the advancement of individuals from a lower class into the higher classes. This is not to say that it is impossible, only that it is very difficult, usually bestowed by Nobles to those who have done a great service to them, or Knights bestow a rank and title of Knighthood on any individual who has proven himself worthy. It is under this elaborate delusion that we discover a truth, the best kind of slave is the one who doesn't even know that they are a slave.

A natural tension exists between the personalities that has played out in the upper class repeatedly over the millennia. Each one seeking control, as they insert their particular influence. In the American political system we watch this happen every four years, during the election campaigns, in an elaborate game of "King of the Mountain[1]," where the object of the game effectively is "to remove the King,"

Israelite history records the chaos of the Book of Judges, the corruption of Israelite leaders, and adds to the foolishness of the people, through 1st Samuel of the Old Testament. The Israelite's internal disintegration, combined with anxiety based on a growing threat from the Philistine army, led them to make a request of Samuel the Prophet. – "Behold, thou art old, and thy sons walk not in thy ways: now make us a king to judge us like all the nations" (1 Sam 8:5).

This natural response to the fear of chaos and the desire to impose order, centralized power, and control is understandable, but it was diametrically opposed to the teachings, faith, and traditions in Israel. Samuel knew that choosing a King would result in what the Israelites had known before - the kingship of Pharaoh in Egypt, who kept them as slaves and he warned them that choosing the way of kingship would be a return to slavery for Israel.

When Israel's elders came to him asking for a king, Samuel responded with very strong words: "This will be the manner of the king that shall reign over you: He will take your sons, and appoint them for himself, for his chariots, and to be his horsemen; and some shall run before his chariots. And he will appoint him captains over thousands, and captains over fifties; and will set them to ear his ground, and to reap his harvest, and to make his instruments of war, and instruments of his chariots. And he will take your daughters to be confectionaries, and to be cooks, and to be bakers. And he will take your fields, and your vineyards, and your oliveyards, even the best of them, and give them to his servants. And he will take the tenth of your seed, and of your vineyards, and give to his officers, and to his servants. And he will take your menservants, and your maidservants, and your goodliest young men, and your asses, and put them to his work. He will take the tenth of your sheep: and ye shall be his servants. And ye shall cry out in that day because of your king which ye shall have chosen you; and the Lord will not hear you in that day (1 Sam

8:11-18).

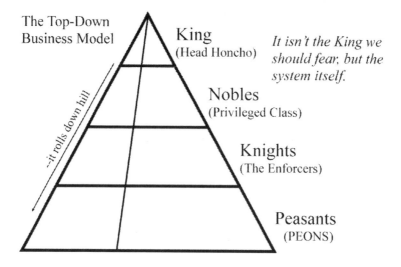

The Top-Down Business Model

...it rolls down hill

King
(Head Honcho)

Nobles
(Privileged Class)

Knights
(The Enforcers)

Peasants
(PEONS)

It isn't the King we should fear, but the system itself.

A simple, yet profound warning that it isn't the King we should fear, but the system itself!

Similarly our Founding Fathers had discovered this general thought as they sought a "new kind of freedom," As early as 1651, the English government had sought to regulate trade in the American colonies. On October 9, the Navigation Acts were passed to ensure that trade enriched only Britain, barring trade with other nations. Some argue that the economic impact was minimal on the colonists, but the political friction which the acts triggered was more serious, as the merchants most directly affected were most politically active. King Philip's War ended in 1678, and much of it was fought without significant assistance from England, which contributed to the development of a unique identity, separate from Britain.

In the 1680s, King Charles II determined to bring the New England colonies under a more centralized administration, in order to regulate trade more effectively. His efforts were fiercely opposed by the colonists, resulting in the abrogation of their colonial charter by the Crown. Charles' successor James II finalized these efforts in 1686, establishing the Dominion of New England. Dominion rule triggered bitter resentment throughout New England; the enforcement of the unpopular Navigation Acts and the curtailing of local democracy angered the colonists. New Englanders were encouraged, however, by a change of government in England that saw James II effectively abdicate, and a populist uprising overthrew Dominion rule on April 18, 1689. Colonial governments reasserted their control in the wake of the revolt, and successive governments made no more attempts to restore the Dominion.

Subsequent English governments continued in their efforts to tax certain goods, passing acts regulating the trade of wool, hats, and molasses. The Molasses Act of 1733 in particular was egregious to the colonists, as a significant part of colonial trade relied on the product. The taxes severely damaged the New England economy, and the taxes were rarely paid as a result, resulting in a surge of smuggling, bribery, and intimidation of customs officials.

The American Revolution was the colonial revolt that took place between 1765 and 1783, when the American Patriots in the Thirteen Colonies won independence from Great Britain, becoming the United States of America. Members of the American colonial society argued the position of "no taxation without representation", starting with the Stamp Act Congress in 1765. They rejected the authority of the British Parliament to tax them because they lacked representation in Parliament. Protests steadily escalated to the burning of the Gaspee in Rhode Island in 1772, followed by the Boston Tea Party in 1773, during which patriots destroyed a consignment of taxed tea. The British responded by closing Boston Harbor, then followed with a series of legislative acts which effectively rescinded Massachusetts Bay Colony's rights of self-government and caused the other colonies to rally behind Massachusetts. In late 1774, the Patriots set up their own alternative government to better coordinate their resistance efforts against Great Britain.

Tensions erupted into battle between Patriot militia and British regulars when the British attempted to capture and destroy colonial military supplies at Lexington and Concord in April 1775. The conflict then escalated into a global war, during which the Patriots (and later their French, Spanish, and Dutch allies) fought the British and Loyalists in what became known as the American Revolutionary War (1775–83). Each of the thirteen colonies formed a Provincial Congress that assumed power from the old colonial governments and suppressed loyalism, and from there they built a Continental Army under the leadership of General George Washington. The Continental Congress determined King George's rule to be tyrannical and infringing the colonists' rights as Englishmen, and they declared the colonies free and independent states on July 2, 1776. The Patriot leadership professed the political philosophies of liberalism and republicanism to reject monarchy and aristocracy, and they proclaimed that all men are created equal. However, not everyone agreed with the new Government and the Revolution, which resulted in the migration of around 60,000 Loyalists to other British territories, especially British North America (Canada).

Among the significant results of the revolution was the creation of the Constitution of the United States, which established a new relatively strong national government, which included three distinct branches, executive, judiciary, and legislature, that represented the states in the Senate and the population in the House of Representatives.

Our Founding Fathers realized that the synergistic cooperation of these branches would result in a balance of the government powers in an open, adaptable, and stable environment, which would equitably represent the people while providing one of the most powerful governing bodies in the world.

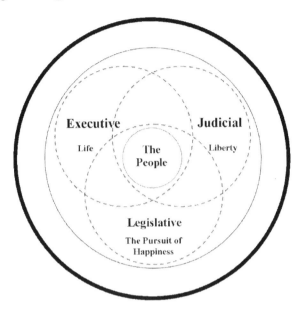

As seen above, traditional leadership generally involves the exercise of power by the one at the "top of the pyramid," By comparison, this inverting of the pyramid results in "Servant Leadership," a phrase coined in an article by Robert K. Greenleaf in 1970, that represents a stewardship philosophy in which the servant-leader shares power, puts the needs of others first, and helps them to develop and perform as effectively as possible. Those who follow this upside down pyramid model champion the change of the organizational mindset, where the leader now exists to serve the people, instead of the people working to serve the leader.

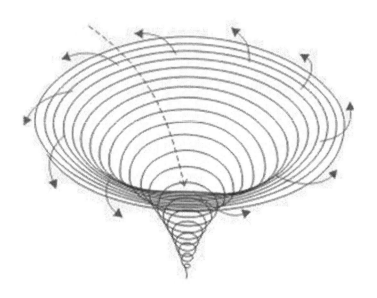

The focus of this inverted pyramid is still at the top, which is of course "the people," However, the power of the people rolls down hill to the executive, and in turn, influence rises up from the executive to the people. This harmonious behavior behaves like a vortex, where the mass of energy (air, gas, water, or fire) spin so swiftly that they pull everything down together toward a central axis or cause. This organizational model has proven itself to be one of the most powerful forces on the earth, and if properly employed, without compulsory means, our desires will naturally flow to us.

Greenleaf states, "When leaders shift their mindset and serve first, they unlock purpose and ingenuity in those around them, resulting in higher performance and engaged, fulfilled employees," He continues, "The servant-leader is servant first... It begins with the natural feeling that one wants to serve, to serve first. Then conscious choice brings one to aspire to lead. That person is sharply different from one who is leader first, perhaps because of the need to assuage an unusual power drive or to acquire material possessions...The leader-first and the servant-first are two extreme types. Between them there are shadings and blends that are part of the infinite variety of human nature.

"The difference manifests itself in the care taken by the servant-first to make sure that other people's highest priority needs are being served. The best test, and difficult to administer, is: Do those served grow as persons? Do they, while being served, become healthier, wiser, freer, more autonomous, more likely themselves to become servants? And, what is the effect on the least privileged in society? Will they benefit or at least not be further deprived?"

Robert Greenleaf recognized that organizations as well as individuals could be servant-leaders. Indeed, he had great faith that servant-leader organizations could change the world. In his second major essay, "The Institution as Servant" (1972,) Greenleaf articulated what is often called the "credo," There he said: "This is my thesis: caring for persons, the more able and the less able serving each other, is the rock upon which a good society is built. Whereas, until recently, caring was largely person to person, now most of it is mediated through institutions – often large, complex, powerful, impersonal; not always competent; sometimes corrupt. If a better society is to be built, one that is more just and more loving, one that provides greater creative opportunity for its people, then the most open course is to raise both the capacity to serve and the very performance as servant of existing major institutions by new regenerative forces operating within them,"

I have all the confidence in the world that if we would choose to realign our government, or build our business enterprises and organizations upon the Servant-Leadership Model, we would find it, just like our Founding Fathers, to be Revolutionary.

[1]King of the mountain was a favored childhood game in which a player attempts to occupy the highest point of a raised platform or hill, while resisting attempts by other players to knock the King off and replace them.

Thomas H. Fairbanks

The Trend is Your Friend?

In my lifetime, we have lived through the "Bay of Pigs incident" with its rehearsal of air raid drills and the huddling in bomb shelters, the assignation and resignation of presidents and the Korean, Vietnam and Desert Storm/Middle East wars, the killing fields of Southeast Asia and the invasions of numerous countries by countless aggressors, extending their political influence, and the toppling of governments. Yet, we have seen miracles like the destruction of the Berlin wall and the seeming end of the Cold War. We have been exposed to the wretchedness of massacres like Kent State, Tiananmen Square, and countless others, along with cruelty, enslavement, and starvation all throughout the world.

Times of crisis create a sense of scarcity. The presumption that life and resources are limited with an accompanying fear that if we don't fight for our share, we'll never get it, and even if we do, it can be taken away from us. The ever increasing rates of domestic violence, abuse and suicide give evidence that many are becoming discouraged with life as they face what appears to be a shallow and pointless existence. Those who espouse this belief learn to live to protect themselves and to hoard all that they can, and as such, economic stability often becomes nothing more than a delicate balance of scarcity.

We have learned by experience, even in this great land, that it is the nature of almost all men, as soon as they think that they obtain a little authority, they will immediately begin to perpetuate this illusion. Using fear, crisis and restrictive regulations, activists boldly solicit acceptance to costly plans and enslaving programs that are designed to demoralize and control, while giving power and prestige to those in authority. Fraud, deceit and waste, coupled with a lack of self-discipline and of a sense of responsibility, which accompany this myth, leaves many individuals trying to survive in the delicate balancing act.

Trends are generally created by four major factors: government, international transactions, speculation/ expectations, and supply & demand. These factors are all intricately linked because our expectation of future conditions shape the decisions we make, and those decisions and expectations influence movements in the marketplace.

The government mainly affects trends through monetary and fiscal policies. Those policies then affect international transactions, which in turn affect economic strength. Speculation and expectations drive prices and demand on what future pricing and acceptance might be. Finally, changes in the supply and demand create recognizable patterns as market participants either accept or reject market conditions. It is by watching these patterns (trends,) which show the shifts in our underlying views, technologies, and knowledge that allows innovators, investors, and traders the opportunity to capture profits.

The underlying drivers of trends can include advances in innovation, scarcity of resources, economic advancement and even changes in consumer tastes. For example, the once booming industries of tapping and farming fur animals almost completely died out because animal activism coupled with consumer choice to wear less expensive synthetic materials for coats and other outerwear. Given the current market acceptance of this change in the marketplace and on-going advances in innovation that offers a wider variety of wearable apparel, it is unlikely that society will reverse this particular trend. Although given the right acceptance, fashion could evolve again into new directions.

Another, more historical, example was the innovation of food transportation by the Union army in the civil war. In an effort to better supply the troops with provisions, a complex logistics mechanism was put in place and, observant innovators took the opportunity to perfect and expand the process of canning food as an easier method to distribute rations to the soldiers. Following the war, this innovation in processing changed food distribution forever because it allowed for an increase of the variety of food choices that could be shipped and made available anywhere.

The period from the end of World War II to the early 1970s was one of the greatest eras of economic expansion in world history. In the US, the Gross Domestic Product increased from $228 billion in 1945 to just under $1.7 trillion in 1975. By then, the US economy represented some 35% of the entire world industrial output, and the US economy was over 3 times larger than that of Japan, the next largest economy.

However, in 1970 an economist by the name of Alan Tofler wrote the book, "Future Shock" and then in 1982 another economist by the name of John Nesbitt wrote his popular book, "Megatrends," It is interesting to note that both of these books discussed the trends the authors had spotted in 1970 and 1982 These are just a few trends - (in my words, not theirs,) which would have an adverse effect on us, and our economy, 30 and 40 years later.

> Number One   - Corporate Instability
> Number Two   - Downsizing
> Number Three - Automation
> Number Four - Mergers & Acquisitions
> Number Five - Asset and Salary Devaluation

The impact that these trends have had on our economy is almost prophetic. For a moment come with me back to 1970, when I was a senior in high school. Do you think anyone talked about corporate instability? Did anybody talk about downsizing? NO! Did anybody talk about automation adversely affecting us? We knew that computers and automation was coming, but we had no idea they were going to replace the workforce! Did we know that companies would, out of necessity, merger together? We hadn't really experienced anything like that before and we never considered that people would actually make careers out of arbitrage or that our assets and salaries would actually lose their value. Surely no one would ever be willing to take a cut in pay to do the same job they had done before. After all, this was America, the home of the free and the land of the brave. Complete with "baseball, hot dogs, apple pie and Chevrolet" (1974 ad campaign created by James Hartzell that *Car and Driver* and other publications ranked as the best automobile commercial of all time).

American Telephone & Telegraph Co. (AT&T) was by and large the largest corporation in the world. AT&T's $26 billion (US) in revenues - the equivalent of $82 billion today - represented 1.4 percent of the U.S. gross domestic product. The next-largest enterprise, General Motors Corp., was one third its size, and was dwarfed by AT&T's $75 billion in assets, nearly one million employees, with more than 100 million customers.

AT&T was a corporate Goliath that seemed as solid as the Rock of Gibraltar. Yet 30 years later, AT&T was almost gone. Of the many events contributing to the company's slippery decline, a crucial one took place on 20 November 1974, the U.S. Department of Justice filed the antitrust suit, resulting from complaints made against AT&T by MCI in their 1974 lawsuit. That lawsuit ended almost a decade later with the breakup of AT&T, and its network known as the Bell System, into seven regional carriers, (that came to be known as the Baby Bells). AT&T retained its long-distance service, along with Bell Telephone Laboratories Inc., its legendary research arm, and the Western Electric Co., its manufacturing subsidiary. From that point on, AT&T had its share of ups and downs. They started new businesses, spun off divisions, and acquired and sold companies, in its efforts to survive, leaving AT&T a shell of what it previously had been.

General Motors (GM) was severely affected by the 1973 oil embargo. Small fuel-efficient cars from foreign automakers took a sharply higher share of the U.S. auto sales market. Under the Energy Policy and Conservation Act, the federal government initiated fuel efficiency standards (known as Corporate Average Fuel Economy, or CAFE) in 1975, effective 1978 for passenger cars, and 1979 for light trucks. For passenger cars, the initial standard was 18 miles per gallon (mpg,) and increased to 27.5 mpg by 1985. GM began responding first to the high gas prices by downsizing most of their models by 1977, but in 1979 as the second oil price spike occurred the economy slid into turmoil, with high inflation, high unemployment, and high interest rates. Sadly, GM, as well as all of the other automakers, suffered large operating losses.

During the 1970s and 1980s all the American auto makers stumbled badly, going from one engineering, manufacturing, or marketing disaster to another. GM had a string of miscues starting with the Chevrolet Vega, which developed a reputation for rapidly rusting and having major problems with the aluminum engine. Cadillac damaged their reputation when the four-cylinder Cadillac Cimarron was introduced in 1981 (a gussied-up Chevrolet Cavalier at twice the price) and the "V8-6-4" engine didn't work as advertised. Their reputation was further damaged when they revealed, in 1977, that they were installing Chevrolet engines in their Oldsmobile models, and lawsuits from aggrieved Oldsmobile owners followed. Likewise litigation ensued when a trio of diesel engines, designed from gasoline engines and used in GM cars from 1978 to 1985 suffered major problems. Class action lawsuits and efforts from the Federal Trade Commission resulted in buybacks of the cars.

In 2005, as oil prices began rising, peaking in 2008, GM was heavily dependent upon the gas-guzzling light truck sales for their profits. As their sales fell sharply, their finance subsidiaries became of greater importance to their overall profitability (and their eventual downfall). Seeking to increase their sustainability, General Motors Acceptance Corporation, the GM finance division, began making home mortgage loans, especially the ill-fated subprime loans and the subsequent collapse of the sub-prime mortgage industry left GM suffering heavy losses, highly leveraged, and burdened by their share of their employee's high health care costs.

With assistance from the Federal Government's Troubled Asset Relief Program (TARP,) GM received a total of $49.5 billion and entered Chapter 11 bankruptcy in June 2009. The U.S. and

Canadian governments received a 72.5% ownership stake, a VEBA (Voluntary Employees Beneficiary Association) received 17.5%, and the unsecured creditors received 10%. As part of the bailout GM, closed numerous production plants, eliminated hundreds of dealerships, and thousands of jobs. They also required a number of major labor union concessions. They sold off the Saab division and eliminated the Pontiac, Hummer, and Saturn Corporation brands. GM received a total of $62 billion from TARP; GMAC, their financing arm, received an additional $17.8 billion. In addition to the funding from the United States government, the Canadian government also provided $10.8 billion to General Motors as an incentive to maintain their production facilities in Canada. Of course, I'm sure you recognize that it is We the People who are going to pay for all of this help from the government!

General Motors is the largest industrial corporation ever to go bankrupt in the United States and the third-largest bankruptcy of any kind, behind the investment bank Lehman Brothers and the telecommunications firm WorldCom.

So, what did these two economists see that the rest of us did not? How did they know what was going to affect us on such a grand scale? How would we have been better off, if only, we had seen these things in advance and taken advantage of that information? There really is a great amount of truth in the saying by that ever-famous, and very popular philosopher, A Nono Mous: "the trend is your friend."

In October of 1973, the Organization of Petroleum Exporting Countries (OPEC) declared an oil embargo upon the supporters of Israel–western nations. The 73-75 recession began immediately after. We were immediately faced with a shortage of oil and gas prices quickly rose to an unheard of rate of $0.55 a gallon. Gasoline had to be rationed and long lines with hour-long waits were commonplace all across the country. Since oil was involved in the manufacturing of plastics, gasoline, sneakers, and almost everything else, the price of oil more than doubled in a just few months from 1973-1974.

Easy-money policies of the American Central Bank, known as the Federal Reserve, which had been designed to generate full employment, coupled with the large spike in the oil price resulted in an out of control rise of the costs of consumer goods; and wages simply could not keep up with the resulting inflation. The energy crisis, inflation and a crisis of leadership in Washington D.C. added up to a devastating recession that ran from November 1973 to March 1975. Interest-sensitive industries, such as housing and automobiles, along with the rising interest rates caused a calamity, which priced many people out of purchasing new cars and homes.

So how did the government react? Upon seeing the poor growth figures of that time period, the Federal Reserve dropped the interest rate in 1973 a full 2% from 11% to around 9%. Rather than sustaining growth, however, the economic band-aid sent inflation into overdrive. Wages could not keep up with the subsequent surge of inflation, purchasing power fell, the hoped for growth did not return, and the stock market crashed loosing 48% of its value.

Terrified by the double-digit inflation rate in 1974, the Federal Reserve switched gears and jacked the interest rate up to nearly 14%. This move wiped out the budding economic recovery. By raising rates again, the economic policy began to starve inflation back down, resulting in a contracted economy, saddled with a very high interest rate. Then the economy slipped back into the throws of the recession for another year or so, and the unemployment rate rose to around 9% by 1975.

Even though the economy came out of the recession in 1975, high unemployment continued to be problematic. In an effort to address unemployment, the Federal Reserve dropped the interest rate in 1975-1976, bottoming out around 5% and it remained fairly stable through 1978. The effort succeeded in bringing unemployment back down to 6%, but inflation started to trend back up.

Then, in 1979, the economy got hit with another oil price shock (this time caused by the Revolution in Iran in January of that year) in which the price of oil more than doubled again, this time resulting in gasoline prices above $0.75 per gallon. This caused another collapse in the economic growth. The Federal Reserve tried again to fight the oil-driven inflation by raising interest rates high into the teens, which peaked out at 20% in 1980. Inflation responded to this economic policy by slumping down to around 10%, but the high interest rates again drove the economy back into recession through the first half of 1980 and unemployment jumped to just under 8%. The Federal Reserve responded again by backing off the interest rate substantially in mid to late 1980, which resulted in a brief return to growth in 1981. But when inflation started rising up above 10%, the Federal Reserve returned to their high interest rate policy in 1981, keeping interest rates above 15% into 1982.

In 1982, oil prices began to decline and inflation was sliding back down. However, the economy moved back into recession and by 1983, the unemployment rate peaked at nearly 11%. To fight this, the Federal Reserve, once again, knocked the interest rate back below 10% and the economic turmoil, which began in 1979, came to a close.

The U.S. Banking Debacle of the 1980s:
A Lesson in Government Mismanagement
As told by Dr. George Kaufman

"Introduction - In the 1980s, the United States experienced its most serious banking crisis since the 1930s and the second most serious crisis in its 200-plus year history. The crisis affected commercial banks, savings banks and savings and loan associations (S&Ls). Between 1980 and 1991, when fundamental corrective laws were enacted, some 1,500 commercial and savings banks (insured by the Federal Deposit Insurance Corporation) and 1,200 savings and loan associations (insured by the former Federal Savings and Loan Insurance Corporation) failed and were resolved by the regulatory agencies. These resolutions represented about 10 percent of all banks at the beginning of the period and 25 percent of all S&Ls. In addition, an even larger number of institutions were in precarious financial condition at some time during this period. The costs of the failures were high, not only to the shareholders of the failed institutions, but also to the surviving institutions, which were required to pay premiums to the deposit insurance agencies, and to U.S. taxpayers, who were forced to make good on the losses after the resources of the S&L insurance fund had been exhausted. For banks, the loss to the FDIC and thus to other solvent banks was about $40 billion. For S&Ls, the loss was near $200 billion, some $150 billion of which was beyond the resources of the FSLIC and was therefore charged to U.S. taxpayers.

"The losses accrued primarily to the federal insurance agencies and taxpayers rather than to depositors and other creditors because the insurance effectively guaranteed the par value of deposits up to $100,000 per account de jure and, except at some small banks, almost any amount of deposits and even borrowings de facto, regardless of the value of the bank's assets. The FDIC and the former FSLIC were funded by premiums imposed on banks and S&Ls, respectively, and both had implicit access to the U.S. Treasury that legislators were unwilling either to challenge or to make explicit until near the end of the debacle.

"The crisis ended in the early 1990s, when interest rates declined, the yield curve turned steeply upward sloping, a series of rolling geographic recessions in various regions of the country came to an end, the aggregate economy slowly expanded, the real estate market bottomed out, and newly adopted legislation increased the cost of poor performance and failure to both the institutions and the regulators. By 1994, both the banking and thrift industries were in their best financial condition since the early 1960s and were realizing record profits. The number of failed and problem institutions declined sharply.

"Background - Banking has always been a volatile industry in the United States, but until the 1930s not an unusual one.[1] The annual failure rate for commercial banks from 1870 to 1913, before the establishment of the Federal Reserve System, averaged 0.78 percent compared to 1.01 percent for nonbanks. The annual volatility of the failure rate was greater for banks, however. The relatively low failure rate existed despite a banking structure that favored failures by restricting banks to one or at best only a few offices, thus preventing them from reducing risk through geographical and product diversification. As a result, the country had thousands of independent banks; the number peaked at 30,000 in the early 1920s. The bank failures increased sharply in the 1920s to near 600 per year, but most of the failures were very small banks. Some 90 percent of the banks had loans and investments of less than $1 million, which adjusted for inflation would be equivalent to only about $10 million currently, and would rank them among the very smallest banks. Their failure had no visible effect on national economic activity. They were primarily located in small agricultural towns in the Midwest. When a recession hit these towns from the rapid fall in farm prices after the post-World War I runup, the local automobile dealer failed, the local drugstore failed, and the local bank failed.

"But things changed dramatically in the 1930s at the onset of the Great Depression. Between 1929 and 1933, the number of banks declined from 26,000 to 14,000, mostly by failure. Indeed, the very first act of newly elected President Franklin D. Roosevelt was to declare a "bank holiday" and close all banks in the country for at least one week in order to prevent depositors from cashing any more of their deposits into currency. The banks were permitted to reopen if the government found them solvent. Thereafter, banking became a relatively stable industry through the late 1970s. The number of bank failures averaged only near 10 per year and the number of S&L failures was not significantly greater. Then the picture changed again.

"Before analyzing the 1980s, it should be noted that both the 1930s and 1980s debacles occurred after the creation of government institutions intended to correct failings in the system that were believed to have been at the root of the problem, and in order to reduce the likelihood of large numbers of simultaneous failures in the future. The Federal Reserve was established in 1913 in the aftermath of sharp jumps in the number of bank failures in 1894 and 1907 in order to increase flexibility in the system. The Fed was to facilitate the flow of bank reserves from capital surplus to capital deficient areas, to provide micro-liquidity through the discount window to individual solvent banks experiencing temporary liquidity problems, and to provide macro-liquidity to the banking system by offsetting outflows of currency and gold. For whatever reasons, not 20 years after it was established, the Fed failed to achieve these objectives sufficiently to prevent the banking crisis of the 1930s, which was far larger, longer, and costlier than any banking crisis before the establishment of the Fed. Indeed, the Fed appears to have introduced greater rigidities at the time of the Great Depression, e.g., prohibiting the issuance of clearing house certificates and making temporary bank suspensions more difficult, than existed before its establishment.[2]

"In large part as a result of the Fed's failure to prevent a recurrence of large-scale bank failures, the FDIC was established in 1934.

While the Fed's decisions to provide liquidity to the banking system in order to offset depositor runs into currency were discretionary, the FDIC operated by rules that effectively eliminated the need for bank runs by unconditionally guaranteeing the par value of insured deposits regardless of the bank's financial condition. This objective was quickly realized and, combined with a more cautious set of bankers and more restrictive regulations imposed by the Banking Act of 1933, the number of bank failures dropped equally quickly and remained low for the next 50 years. However, as was true of the Federal Reserve's structure, flaws eventually appeared in the FDIC that in time led to increases in bank failures that matched the conditions in the 1930s before the introduction of deposit insurance.

"The S&L Debacle[3] - Savings and loan institutions are traditional residential mortgage lenders. Before the introduction of deposit insurance in 1934, S&Ls made primarily intermediate three-to-five-year renewable mortgage loans. These loans were effectively variable rate mortgages with sizeable down payments. They were financed by time deposits (legally labeled share capital,) which were not necessarily redeemable on demand. As a result, neither the S&Ls' interest rate nor liquidity exposures were very great.

"But things changed dramatically after 1934. Public policy encouraged S&Ls to make progressively longer-term (first 20, then 25, and finally 30-year) fixed-rate mortgages with progressively smaller down payments. At the same time, the new deposit insurance program effectively increased the liquidity and shortened the maturity of their deposits. These changes increased the institutions' exposure to interest rate and liquidity risk. Indeed, the large degree of maturity (duration) mismatch by the mid1970s made the industry a disaster waiting to happen.

"When interest rates increased sharply in the late 1970s as a result of inflation, the disaster occurred. Between 1976 and 1980, interest rates on three-month Treasury bills jumped from 4 percent to 16 percent and those on long-term Treasury securities from 6 percent to 13 percent. By 1982, an estimated 85 percent of all S&Ls were losing money and two-thirds were economically or market value insolvent so that, ceteris paribus, they would be unable to pay their depositors in full and on time. The negative economic net worth of the industry and the corresponding loss to the FSLIC was generally estimated to be about $100 billion,[4] although some estimates placed it as high as $150 billion. This figure represents the difference between the par value of deposit accounts (the large majority of which were less than the maximum insured $100,000 per account) at insolvent institutions and the market value of the S&Ls' assets. But the FSLIC resolved only a very small number of the insolvencies for a number of reasons, including:[5]

- It was overwhelmed by the large number of insolvencies, and its staff was far too small and unprepared to deal with the crisis,

- It had insufficient reserves to cover the deficits at insolvent institutions and pay off depositors at par, whether the institutions were sold, merged or liquidated,

- Formal recognition of the large losses would be a black mark on the agency's record,

- Formal recognition of the large losses and number of insolvencies might spread fear among the public and ignite a run on all institutions that would spill over to commercial banks and even beyond to the macro-economy. Further,

- Many of the losses were "only" unrecognized paper losses; and, because interest rates are cyclical and there was a high probability that they would decline again in the not very distant future, it was hoped that waiting would restore the associations to economic solvency.

"Therefore, regulators publicly denied the magnitude of the problem, argued that the problem was a liquidity rather than a solvency problem, introduced creative accounting measures to make the industry's net worth appear higher even than the already overstated book value levels (i.e., they covered up the evidence,) delayed imposing sanctions on insolvent and near-insolvent institutions, and encouraged institutions to reduce their interest rate exposure by using newly permitted variable-rate mortgages and shorter-term loans to reduce their maturity mismatch. And the regulators and the industry lucked out. Interest rates declined sharply from 1982 through 1986. This reversal in rates caused the industry's net worth to rise and by 1985 its estimated negative net worth was only about $25 billion and was expected to improve further, ceteris paribus ("all other things being equal.")

"But ceteris did not remain paribus for many institutions. A substantial number incurred increases in credit risk that offset the decline in interest rate risk and either prevented their net worth from increasing greatly or actually caused it to decline further. The assumption of credit risk was either unintentional, arising from severe local and regional economic recessions, or intentional, arising from calculated gambles to regain solvency.

"The first and most severe regional recessions started in the mid-1980s in Texas and the neighboring energy-producing states in the Southwest following the collapse of world oil prices. This area had experienced a strong economic surge based on sharply rising oil prices and expectations of continued price increases. Employment, income, and real estate values all increased sharply and stimulated both a rapid immigration of people in search of employment and a building boom, particularly in commercial real estate. Much of this boom was financed by local S&Ls. When oil prices not only failed to increase further after 1981, but declined sharply from $30 a barrel in 1985 to near $10 in 1986, the bubble burst.[6] As incomes and real estate values dropped, borrowers defaulted on loans, and collateral values fell too fast for many lending S&Ls to protect the value of all their loans. As a result, many S&Ls became insolvent.

"At the same time, a number of institutions, particularly those that had only recently converted from mutual ownership (which was the prevailing form of ownership) to stock ownership in order to raise additional capital more easily, became tempted to "gamble for resurrection,) Because these institutions had little if any market value capital of their own to lose, this was a logical strategy. If the high-risk bets paid off, the institution won and possibly regained solvency. If the institution lost, the FSLIC bore the loss. That is, heads the institution won, tails the FSLIC lost! Some S&Ls placed progressively larger bets on the table by offering above market interest rates on deposits so that their deposit size grew rapidly. Such gambling was often accompanied by fraud, either ex-ante deliberate or ex-ante inadvertent through excessive carelessness in extending and monitoring loans. Particularly at the more rapidly growing associations, loan documentation was frequently incomplete or even nonexistent, recordkeeping was casual at best, and loan collection was sporadic and done with little enthusiasm. Some of the new owners were land developers, who are gamblers almost by nature. They used greatly overinflated values of their personal properties as the base for their institution's capital, and the resources of the institution as their personal "piggy banks" to finance their ventures. Losses were often not recognized on the institutions' books on a complete or timely basis, so that the institutions gave false appearances of solvency.

"The National Commission appointed in 1992 to identify and examine the origins and causes of the S&L debacle concluded that: "It is difficult to overstate the importance of accounting abuses in aggravating and obscuring the developing debacle. It would have been difficult for the process to continue for so long in the absence of an information structure that obscured the extent of the mounting losses,)[7] The FSLIC economic deficit (computed as the difference between the par value of insured deposits at economically insolvent S&Ls and the market value of their assets,) which had declined from some $100 billion in 1982 to near $25 billion in 1985, climbed back up to above $100 billion in 1989, almost entirely due to losses from credit risk exposure.

"Commercial banks were not as badly hit by the interest rate increase in the late 1970s because the maturities on the two sides of their balance sheets were not as mismatched. But, like the S&Ls, they experienced large credit losses in the mid and late 1980s that resulted in the largest number of bank failures since the 1930s and the second largest number in U.S. history. These losses threatened to bankrupt the FDIC.

"Structured Early Intervention and Resolution and Deposit Insurance Reform - The S&L and bank problems were in large part caused by deposit insurance. The structure of deposit insurance adopted in 1933 had both good and bad aspects. The good aspect effectively prevented a systemwide run from deposits into currency by guaranteeing the par value of most deposits. Thus, it prevented the type of reserve drain experienced in the United States in the early 1930s.

"The bad aspects were, first, that this guarantee reduced, if it did not eliminate, the incentive for many depositors to monitor the financial performances of their banks and thus encouraged both a moral hazard problem for banks and a principal-agent problem for regulators. Bank managers/owners, knowing that few if any depositors were looking over their shoulders and that their insurance premiums were not scaled to their risk exposure, deliberately or inadvertently assumed greater risks either by increasing the credit and interest rate risk exposures in their portfolios and/or by decreasing their capital-asset ratios more than they would have in the absence of insurance. Bank regulators, knowing that most depositors had little if any incentive to flee financially troubled banks, were then able to delay imposing sanctions on troubled institutions and even resolving insolvent institutions, thereby keeping them in operation. To the extent that these institutions increased their losses, the regulators' principals–healthy, premium-paying institutions and taxpayers–were not well served.[8]

"In an attempt to solve the problem, Congress at year-end 1991 enacted the FDIC Improvement Act (FDICIA,) which focuses on Structured Early Intervention and Resolution (SEIR). SEIR reforms deposit insurance by attempting to impose on insured depository institutions the same conditions that the private market imposes on firms not covered by federal insurance whose financial condition is deteriorating, including conditions that the banks themselves impose on their borrowers. Moreover, it attempts to resolve troubled institutions before their own capital turns negative. Thus, losses would accrue only to shareholders, not to depositors, and deposit insurance would effectively be redundant.

"SEIR's objective is also to reduce the discretion of regulators by imposing more specific rules, thus reducing the power of regulators. As such, it resembles the partial replacement of Federal Reserve discretion by FDIC insurance rules following the Fed's failure to prevent the banking crisis and economic depression of the early 1930s.[9] To protect their power, the regulators successfully fought to weaken many of the provisions reducing their discretionary authority during the legislative processing leading to the enactment of FDICIA and continued to weaken the potential effectiveness of the Act further by drafting weak regulations to implement it.[10]

"The Lesson - An analysis of the experience of the U.S. banking debacle of the 1980s suggests that to minimize the moral hazard problem federally insured depository institutions should be subjected to the same conditions imposed by the private market on noninsured firms and that to minimize the regulators' principal-agent problem the insurer and other bank regulatory agencies should be required to operate in a transparent manner, be prohibited from providing forbearance, and be held fully accountable for their actions and inactions.

"The major source of both the instability in the U.S. banking system in the 1980s that resulted in the exceptionally large number of bank and S&L failures and the associated large losses was not the private sector but the public or government sector. The government first created many of the underlying causes of the problem by forcing S&Ls to assume excessive interest rate risk exposure and preventing both S&Ls and banks from minimizing their credit risk exposure through optimal product and geographic diversification and then delayed in applying solutions to the problem by granting forbearance to economically insolvent or near-insolvent institutions. That is, the banking debacle was primarily an example of government failure rather than market failure,)

1. A brief history and additional references appear in George J. Benston, Robert A. Eisenbeis, Paul M. Horvitz, Edward J. Kane and George G. Kaufman, Perspectives of

Safe and Sound Banking, Cambridge, Mass.: MIT Press, 1986, Chapter 2.

2. Milton Friedman and Anna J. Schwartz, A Monetary History of the United States 1867-1960, Princeton, N.J.: Princeton University Press, 1963, Chapter 7.

3. Although savings banks have more in common with S&Ls than commercial banks, because they were insured by the FDIC rather than the FSLIC, data on them is included with that for commercial banks.

4. See Bert Ely, "Savings and Loan Crisis" in David R. Henderson, ed- Fortune Encyclopedia of Economics, New York: Warner Books, 1993, p. 72.

5. Edward J. Kane, The Gathering Crises in Federal Deposit Insurance, Cambridge, Mass.: MIT Press, 1985; The S&L Insurance Mess: How Did It Happen? Washington, D.C.: Urban Institute Press, 1989, James R. Barth, The Great Savings and Loan Debacle, Washington, D.C.: American Enterprise Institute, 1991; George G. Kaufman, "The Savings and Loan Rescue of 1989: Causes and Perspective" in George G. Kaufman, ed., Restructuring the American Financial System. Boston: Kluwer Academic, 1990; George J. Benston and George G. Kaufman, "Understanding the Savings and Loan Debacle," The Public Interest, Spring, 1990, pp. 79-95; National Commission on Financial Institution Reform, Recovery and Enforcement, Origins and Causes of the S&L Debacle: A Blueprint for Reform—Report to the President and Congress of the United States, Washington, D.C., July 1993; Martin Lowy, High Rollers: Inside the Savings and Loan Debacle, New York. Praeger, 1991; and Martin Mayer, The Greatest Ever Bank Robbery: The Collapse of the Savings and Loan Industry. New York: Charles Scribner, 1990.

6. Paul M. Horvitz, "The Collapse of the Texas Thrift Industry" in George 0. Kaufman, ed., Restructuring the

American Financial System, Kluwer, 1990, pp. 95-116.

7. National Commission, p. 9.

8. Edward J. Kane, "Changing Incentives Facing Financial-Services Regulators," Journal of Financial Services Research. September 1989, pp. 265-274 and Edward J. Kane, "How Market Forces Influence the Structure of Financial Regulation" in William S. Haraf and Rose Marie Kushmeider, eds., Restructuring Banking and Financial Services in America, Washington, D.C.: American Enterprise Institute, 1988, pp. 343-382.

9. The battle between rules and discretion in banking regulation resembles the more publicized and longer-run battle between rules and discretion in the conduct of monetary policy carried on in the U. S. at least since the 1930s.

10. George J. Benston and George G. Kaufman, "Improving the FDIC Improvement Act: What Was Done and What Still Needs to be Done to Fix the Deposit Insurance Problem" in George G. Kaufman, ed., Reforming Financial Institutions and Markets in the United States, Boston; Kluwer Academic, 1994, pp. 99-120; and Kenneth E. Scott and Barry R. Weingast, "Banking Reform: Economic Propellants, Political Impediments" in George G. Kaufman, ed., Reforming Financial Institutions and Markets in the United States, 1994, pp. 19-36.

[The Author, Dr. Kaufman, is the John Smith Professor of Banking and Finance at Loyola University of Chicago, and is Co-Chair of the Shadow Financial Regulatory Committee. This paper is a shortened version of a longer paper presented at the International Conference on Bad Enterprise Debts in Central and Eastern Europe in Budapest, Hungary on June 6-8, 1994. The article is at: https://fee.org/articles/the-us-banking-debacle-of-the-1980s-a-lesson-in-government-mismanagement/]

Thomas H. Fairbanks

Cures & Loopholes

In the 1980s, money market accounts with banks became more and more popular because they offered higher interest rates on savings accounts without FSLIC insurance coverage. When S&L depositors moved their deposits, it depleted the S&L's source of funds. S&Ls then asked Congress to remove their mandated low interest rate restrictions and the Carter Administration allowed S&Ls to raise interest rates on savings deposits and also raised the FSLIC insurance level from $40,000 to $100,000 per depositor.

By 1982, S&Ls were losing $4 billion a year, which was a radical decline from their profits in 1980 at $781 million. In 1982, President Reagan signed the Garn-St. Germain Depository Institutions Act, which solidified the elimination of the interest rate cap and it also permitted the S&Ls to have up to 40 percent of their assets in commercial loans and 30 percent in consumer loans. The law removed restrictions on loan-to-value ratios and gave the S&Ls permission to use federally-insured deposits to make risky loans. At the same time, budget cuts reduced the regulatory staff at the FHLBB, which impaired the ability to investigate bad loans. Between 1982 and 1985, S&L assets increased by 56 percent. Legislators in California, Texas and Florida passed laws allowing their S&Ls to invest in speculative real estate, which allowed S&Ls in Texas to triple in size. Despite these laws, 35 percent of the country's S&Ls still weren't profitable by 1983 and nine percent were technically bankrupt. As banks went under, the FSLIC started running out of funds. For that reason, the government allowed bad S&Ls to remain open. They continued to make bad loans and the losses kept mounting. In 1987, the FSLIC fund declared itself insolvent by $3.8 billion. Congress kicked the can down the road by recapitalizing it in May. But that just delayed the inevitable. In 1989, the newly-elected President George H.W. Bush unveiled his bailout plan. The Financial Institutions Reform, Recovery and Enforcement Act provided $50 billion to close failed banks and stop further losses. It set up a new government agency called the Resolution Trust Corporation to resell bank assets. The proceeds were used to pay back depositors. FIRREA also changed S&L regulations to help prevent further poor investments and fraud.

As it has been said before, Real Estate gambling during, and after the S&L crisis was often accompanied by fraud, either deliberate or inadvertent, through excessive carelessness in extending and monitoring loans. Particularly at the more rapidly growing associations, loan documentation was frequently incomplete or even nonexistent, recordkeeping was casual at best, and loan collection was sporadic and done with little enthusiasm. Some of the new owners were land developers, who are gamblers almost by nature. They used greatly overinflated values of their personal properties as the base for their institution's capital, and the resources of the institution as their personal "piggy banks" to finance their ventures.

The vast majority of real estate professionals (i.e. real estate brokers and agents, mortgage brokers, lender reps, mortgage underwriters, appraisers, escrow and title officers) perform their assignments ethically and properly. Some however, wittingly or unwittingly, have been party to faulty or fraudulent mortgage transactions simply because they are operating under Standard Industry Practices.

Fraud is defined as "Intentional misrepresentation or concealment of information in order to deceive or mislead," (dictionary.university/fraud) It is a willful intent that is both immoral and illegal. There are basically two kinds of fraudulent activities associated with real estate. 1) Real Estate & Mortgage

Scams, which are primarily aimed at taking advantage of an individual or group of individuals in a related real estate transaction. 2) Mortgage Fraud, which is primarily focused on taking advantage of the lending institutions, independently or collectively with the other individual participants in a real estate transaction.

Real Estate & Mortgage Scams Some common types of Real Estate Scams include "predators" who actively seek out homeowners, typically senior citizens, who have significant equity in their homes. The goal is to steal the homeowner's equity through whatever fraud, misrepresentation, flimflam, trick or device is available. The tools of the trade include telemarketing, flyers, billboards, home improvement contracts with built-in security agreements, door-to-door salesmen offering deals that "sound too good to be true," small print, outright lies, high interest loans, high loan fees and the balloon payments, and shoddy construction.

Once the predators finish their work, the "scavengers" appear. Just like on the Serengeti, scavengers finish up after the predator has made the "kill,) Scavengers include "foreclosure specialists", bankruptcy mills, and lenders who take advantage of the victim through high interest rates, points and huge loan fees. While offering hope to the victim, they take the victim's last few dollars and foreclose on the property. The media often reports that this type of scavenger is employing "predatory lending practices."

As if the predators and scavengers were not enough! "Forgers" and "Identity Thieves" are hard at work forging quitclaim deeds, notary stamps and signatures, loan applications, real estate appraisals, employment histories, tax returns, and credit histories. They target lenders who fail to exercise good quality control or who stoically accept fraud losses as a "cost of doing business". Unfortunately, we all pay for the fraud through higher interest, higher fees, higher title insurance cost, and the "dreaded" Private Mortgage Insurance. They do not work alone and will often enlist law-abiding people to aid and abet their crimes.

Anyone who has ever owned a home knows that the purchase of

that home may have been one of the most important purchases they ever made. However, how would you, as a homeowner, feel if you discovered the house that you purchased was stolen from you without your knowledge? Some transfers of real property were, in fact, based on fraud or forged deeds. The criminals involved in these types of transfers are quite familiar with real estate transactions and can steal a home, borrow against it and flee with the money long before the true homeowner or even the mortgage companies ever become aware of it.

Mortgage Fraud There are two basic types of mortgage fraud: 1) There's the type where someone falsifies information to get an application approved. 2) Then there's the kind in which an organized ring systematically fleeces lending institutions through orchestrated schemes. Backed by phony professionals, crooks buy and sell homes rapidly at greatly inflated prices, then pocket the loan money.

"Why rent when you can own your own home?" a Pennsylvania builder asked in a television advertisement in New York. Why indeed? Especially when the same company was offering to pay a buyer's rent for a full year, so they could save for the down payment.

Fleeing the city to join the other 170 new homeowners in the Pocono Mountains, the Danny Ruiz family purchased a three-bedroom Cape Cod in 1999 for $171,000. But when they tried to refinance less than two years later, the home was valued at just $125,000.

How could their home have lost so much of its value, in a time of rising real-estate prices? The Pennsylvania Attorney General's theory is "an inflated appraisal". State officials have sued an appraiser and the builder, claiming they colluded to sell the inflated Pocono property. The state has also launched a criminal investigation.

This case was part of a widening assault on the mortgage industry, with consumer advocates, mortgage companies and even appraisers questioning the integrity of the real estate valuation and mortgage process.

Once again, federal prosecutors focused on inflated-appraisal schemes as part of an effort to root out mortgage fraud, which had risen sharply in recent years. Congress began revisiting regulation of appraisers for the first time since enactment of FIRREA, which resulted from the savings-and-loan debacle of the 1980s.

Appraisers were finding themselves defendants in lawsuits arising from home loans that have gone bad and under automatic suspicion, from within their own industry due to a growing sentiment that "one is guilty until proven innocent."

This type of unethical behavior exposed the shaky foundations of the hot housing market in the new millennium. Spurred by low interest rates, mortgage lending rose 19% to a record $2.4 trillion. But with the economy stuck in low gear and sales slowing, many experts feared home prices would soon drop. Substantial blame fell on the nation's 40,000 residential appraisers, just as Wall Street securities analysts were being criticized for hyping overpriced stocks before the Internet bubble burst.

With all of the regulation foresight, Congress hadn't planned on a major shift in lending industry practices. Very few of the people involved in making mortgage loans had a long-term interest in them. Traditionally, bankers had made loans directly and held them, giving the lenders a strong incentive to protect their interests.

Independent mortgage brokers, who were paid per transaction and had little stake in the long-term health of the loans were responsible for choosing the various mortgage service providers needed to close a mortgage transaction (i.e. appraisers, processors, credit reporting agency, title and escrow companies.) Several lenders had also lost a long-term interest in their loans because they could sell them off to investors with a favorable return long before the first mortgage payment came due.

Appraisers increasingly feared that if they didn't produce the inflated valuations, that were often sought by brokers, that their business would dry up, said a spokesman for the Appraisal Institute. More than 7,000 appraisers had also signed a petition saying they had been subjected to customer pressure and called on regulators to forbid the practice.

Predatory Lending Scams So, why was this allowed to happen? The White Collar Crime statistics reported typically omitted the real estate sector and real estate loan frauds. There were no good statistics available due to lender segregation and an aversion to reporting. (The Mortgage Bankers Association represented only one segment of the lending industry in the US. Not all mortgage companies were members of the MBA, and not all members report. In addition, the banks, thrifts, finance companies and credit unions all had their own statistics, which were not a part of the public domain.) It was speculated, however, that Mortgage Fraud alone could be an additional $120 billion. The MBA alone reported an increase from $60 billion to $70 billion per year back in 2003.

Part of the problem was an aversion by regulated lenders to admit to Mortgage Fraud. If a regulated institution reported loan fraud, its reserves would be affected, audits triggered and the institution's ratings and stock price would be adversely impacted.

Financially speaking, there were profits to be made in funding fraudulent loans. This is especially true with the growth of the Sub-Prime sector of the mortgage industry. Loans to "A" credit borrowers, with good equity, provide the lowest yields in terms of rates and fees. While loans to "B", "C", or "D" credit borrowers, or those with low equity, generated much higher rates and fees.

This is shown in the following example on a $100,000 fixed rate, 30-year mortgage:

Credit Rating	Interest Rate	Points	Fees	Total Fees Collected
A	6.75	1-1.5	$2,500	$3,500-$4,000
B	8.00	2.5-5	$4,000	$6,500-$9,000

| C | 10.00 | 5-10 | $6,000 | $11-$16,000 |
| D | 12.00 | 10-20 | $8,000 | $18-$28,000 |

The stock price of publicly traded lending institutions were enhanced when their fee income was a large portion of their total income, and when their interest income had a higher spread than their costs of funds rate (the average rate paid on savings deposits). Remember, loan production managers and executives received bonuses based on profits.

Booking loans that were Packed with 5-15 extra points, plus an almost equal amount of garbage fees, was a good thing, good for business. Unless, of course, it was Grandma's house and they just stole her equity.

It is easy to see why Predatory Lending became a topic before the Senate Permanent Investigations Committee, as well as various state legislatures, counties and cities. In Ohio, the Organized Crime Commission also investigated these problems.

Flipping Real Estate Scams The act of buying real property for a low price and selling the same property for market value is a long established legal practice. The flipping, or quick turn over of a property in itself is not always an illegal act, as it depends on the circumstances. The sale must be fair and to achieve fairness the following conditions must be met: 1) Buyers and sellers are typically motivated; 2) both parties are well informed or well advised, and acting in what they consider their best interests; 3) The price represents consideration for the property sold unaffected by special or creative financing, or sale concessions granted by anyone associated with the sale.

A flip can be considered legal if someone bought a home, fixed it up within a few weeks, then sold it for a profit; or if someone needing to sell due to a variety of motivations such as a quick move out of town because of a job transfer, and sold a home for less than market value, only to see it resold immediately for its real market value.

The majority of flipping cases involve residential properties (One to Four Family Units). An illegal flip is one in which an inflated appraisal or another deception is used to obtain a mortgage.

An example of an illegal flip could be as described: A buyer contracts to purchase a property in their name for $90,000 (its real market value) but before closing the deal draws up a second contract to sell the property to another buyer at $130,000 (a price that is substantially higher than the real market value). Then they look for financing for the second contract through a loan officer or mortgage broker, who, using their persuasive influence, finds an appraiser to fraudulently inflate the value of the property enough to justify the loan while being compensated with an unusually high appraisal fee. Once the lender approves the loan package and releases the $130,000, the contracts are closed either simultaneously or within a few days or weeks of each other. The original contract is paid off and the schemer divides the remaining funds ($40,000) between himself and any other co-conspirators (usually the mortgage broker or loan officer and sometimes the second buyer.)

The scheme's design generally has nothing to do with the ownership and use of the property, other than for the purpose of obtaining mortgage funds. The buyer may or may not make a few payments on the property, then allow it to go into foreclosure. Only then does the unsuspecting lender discover that the property's value does not cover the value of the loan.

Flipping reached its greatest profit level in the FHA loan programs, especially on the 2-4 units loans. Because 97% loans can be obtained (along with costs and fees that are added to the loan,) the profits are higher than on conventional loans that have lower loan ratios.

It had been reported from a metropolitan area that several four-plex units with a real market value in the $140,000-$160,000 range, were being flipped at the $330,000 range. Using $150,000 as an average real market value, the profit margin was $180,000 per deal. One Fraud Ring did over 30 flips within one neighborhood alone. Look at the numbers, $180,000 x 30 = $5,400,000 in excess profits, in one neighborhood, by one small group. In this case, they were operating so long in the area that they have even bought back the same property after it was foreclosed on and flipped it again. In other cases, they had flipped the same property three times in four years, buying it back out of foreclosure and duping yet another lender. Kind of makes you wonder if either they are really smart or the lenders and the appraisers are really stupid or blind. Of course, by now maybe it really is market value.

Although flipping is only one type of real estate fraud, other typical techniques are used in the process. Some of them are laid out in a 116 count, federal grand jury indictment of Robert A. Amico, his sons, and various associates in a case of alleged, extensive mortgage fraud in the Rochester, New York area. Amico and fellow defendants are accused of defrauding banks of $58.5 million.

Amico and associates (using over a dozen company names) built, sold and arranged financing for some 230 homes in Rochester's suburbs. The sales price of over half was far above assessed value. In one suburb alone, Amico built 21 percent of tax delinquent properties.

The grand jury indictment of Amico outlined a "conspiracy" in which the defendants falsified mortgage applications using bogus documentation. The falsified mortgage applications hid the fact that purchasers would not qualify financially for the loan.

Many of the purchasers were not so seemingly innocent. To quickly attract the many purchasers needed to purchase the homes built by the Amico Entities, purchasers were able to buy the homes with no out-of-pocket expenses. Specifically, the purchasers were not required to pay a down payment, closing costs or attorney's fees. And many of the purchasers were offered large cash rebates to buy the homes.

The defendants falsely represented to the lenders that the sales prices for the homes were in amounts which were much greater than the actual sales prices paid by the purchasers and documents were prepared which falsely represented that the purchasers provided down payments of approximately 20 to 25 percent of the purported sales prices - a down payment, however, that was never paid by the purchaser.

To support phony sales prices, the defendants deceived various property appraisers by providing: a) blueprints, which falsely inflated the square footage of the homes, b) purchase agreements which falsely stated that the purchasers had agreed to pay the inflated sales price for the homes; and/or c) information regarding comparable sales of other Amico homes in which the value of those properties had been inflated. The defendants also altered legitimate appraisals and created false appraisals using the names of real estate appraisers who did not exist.

Mortgage fraud has the power to distort markets and undermine neighborhoods. The suburban towns where Amico built relied on the same dummied up blue prints when appraising the properties for tax purposes. Artificially inflated values result in tax delinquencies and foreclosures. In inner cities, flipped properties are often abandoned by those unable or unwilling to make the oppressive mortgage payments. Abandoned buildings frequently become eyesores or pass into the hands of absentee landlords to become strip mine rental properties and drug warrens. Some buildings are flipped again and again. Hitting bottom, then bobbing back up for a new round of grab the money and run.

No one can dispute the claim that abuse and collusion are a reality, and there is ample evidence to place blame across the board. Each player in the Amico mortgage fraud case claims everyone had a little piece of responsibility. An all too familiar claim in matters of fraud. Spreading participation around gives more people a stake in the cover-up and makes the unraveling tougher. With mortgage fraud, the difficulty is compounded by the increasingly layered nature of mortgage transactions. The farther a transaction gets from its point of origin, the more difficult it becomes to scrutinize.

Some suggest that the bundling and resale of loans as mortgage-backed securities had been an important factor in the growth of mortgage fraud, as have online and automated mortgage procedures. Plus, it was common for mortgages issued by one company to end up being bought by a string of others. Some companies took advantage of the opportunities this presented for fraud. Records of payments got "lost" or payments were misapplied, resulting in fees and in some cases, foreclosure.

It was simply another form of flipping - the mortgage company gets the equity and property and puts the home back into the moneymaking pipeline. Individual homeowners with tight budgets found it too difficult to fight an out-of-state mortgage company, particularly the ones who had raised obfuscation to an art form.

Culprits

The 1989 failure of a small Arkansas savings and loan, Madison Guaranty Savings & Loan, triggered criminal probes which targeted some of President Bill Clinton's oldest friends and political allies, compelling the President repeatedly to deny allegations that he had a role in the debacle. A March 1992 New York Times article published during the 1992 U.S. presidential campaign reported that the Clintons, then governor and first lady of Arkansas, had invested and lost money in the failed Whitewater Development Corporation who had defaulted on loans with the failed S&L.

There are several ways in which the Bush family played into the Savings and Loan scandal, which involves not only many members of the Bush family, but also many other politicians who were part of the Bush Jr. administration. Jeb Bush, George Bush Sr., and his son Neil Bush had all been implicated in the Savings and Loan Scandal, which cost American tax payers over $1.4 TRILLION dollars. Jeb Bush defaulted on a $4.56 million loan from Broward Federal Savings in Sunrise, Florida. After federal regulators closed the S&L, the office building that Jeb financed using the $4.56 million, was reappraised by the regulators at $500,000, which Bush and his partners paid. The taxpayers had to pay back the remaining 4 million plus dollars.

Neil Bush was the most widely targeted member of the Bush family by the press in the S&L scandal. Neil became director of Silverado Savings and Loan at the age of 30 in 1985. Three years later the institution was belly up at a cost of $1.6 billion to tax payers to bail out. The basic actions of Neil Bush in the S&L scandal are as follows: Neil received a $100,000 "loan" from Ken Good, of Good International, with no obligation to pay any of the money back. Good was a large shareholder in JNB Explorations, Neil Bush's oil-exploration company. Neil failed to disclose this conflict-of-interest when loans were given to Good from Silverado, because the money was to be used in joint venture with his own JNB. This was in essence giving himself a loan from Silverado through a third party. Neil then helped Silverado S&L approve Good International for a $900,000 line of credit. Good defaulted on a total $32 million in loans from Silverado. During this time Neil Bush did not disclose that $3 million of the $32 million that Good was defaulting on was actually for investment in JNB, his own company. Good subsequently raised Bush's JNB salary from $75,000 to $125,000 and granted him a $22,500 bonus. Neil Bush maintained that he did not see how this constituted a conflict of interest. Neil approved $106 million in Silverado loans to another JNB investor, Bill Walters. Neil also never formally disclosed his relationship with Walters and Walters also defaulted on his loans, all $106 million of them. Neil Bush was charged with criminal wrongdoing in the case and ended up paying $50,000 to settle out of court. The chief of Silverado S&L was sentenced to 3.5 years in jail for pleading guilty to $8.7 million in theft. (For more see: ww.rationalrevolution.net/war/bush_family_and_the_s.htm)

The Keating Five were five United States Senators accused of corruption in 1989, igniting a major political scandal as part of the larger Savings and Loan crisis of the late 1980s and early 1990s. The five senators – Alan Cranston (Democrat of California,) Dennis DeConcini (Democrat of Arizona,) John Glenn (Democrat of Ohio,) John McCain (Republican of Arizona,) and Donald W. Riegle, Jr. (Democrat of Michigan) – were accused of improperly intervening in 1987 on behalf of Charles H. Keating, Jr., Chairman of the Lincoln Savings and Loan Association, which was the target of a regulatory investigation by the Federal Home Loan Bank Board (FHLBB). The FHLBB subsequently backed off taking action against Lincoln.

Lincoln Savings and Loan collapsed in 1989, at a cost of over $3 billion to the federal government. Some 23,000 Lincoln bondholders were defrauded and many investors lost their life savings. The substantial political contributions Keating had made to each of the senators, totaling $1.3 million, attracted considerable public and media attention. After a lengthy investigation, the Senate Ethics Committee determined in 1991 that Cranston, DeConcini, and Riegle had substantially and improperly interfered with the FHLBB's investigation of Lincoln Savings, with Cranston receiving a formal reprimand. Senators Glenn and McCain were cleared of having acted improperly but were criticized for having exercised "poor judgment". (Wikipedia reference)

The House banking scandal broke in early 1992, when it was revealed that the United States House of Representatives allowed members to overdraw their House checking accounts without risk of being penalized by the House bank (actually a clearinghouse). The scandal ultimately involved more than 450 representatives, most of whom did not break any laws. Twenty-two congressmen and women were singled out by the House Ethics Committee for leaving their checking accounts overdrawn for at least eight months out of a sample of 39 months. The scandal contributed to a perception of corruption and malfeasance and was a contributing factor to major changes in the House, in which 77 Representatives resigned or were ousted in the 1994 election. Four ex-Congressmen, a Delegate, and the former House Sergeant at Arms were convicted of wrongdoing as a result of the investigation that followed. Among these, former Rep. Buz Lukens (R-OH) was convicted on bribery and conspiracy charges. Former Rep. Carl C. Perkins (D-KY) pleaded guilty to various charges including a check kiting scheme involving several financial institutions including the House Bank. Former Rep. Carroll Hubbard (D-KY) pleaded guilty to three felonies. The former Sergeant at Arms, Jack Russ, pleaded guilty to three felonies. (Wikipedia reference)

It does make one wonder how foolish "we, the people" have been in allowing those we elect to protect and serve us to become the fox who guards the hen house?

USU - *Weathering the Financial Storm*

In the third quarter of 2008 the US Government made one of the biggest bailouts in history to many of the largest financial institutions in the world that had experienced severe losses resulting from the collapse in the subprime mortgage market and the resulting credit crisis, the likes of which had not been seen since the Great Depression. Multi-billion dollar banks collapsed, the Stock Market dropped by nearly 50%, and unemployment skyrocketed to over 10%. Banks, which had been providing an increasing number of mortgages to borrowers with low credit scores, experienced massive loan losses when many of these "special affordable" mortgages went into default. As well-known financial institutions like Countrywide, Lehman Brothers and Bear Stearns began failing, the government responded with the Troubled Asset Relief Program (TARP). The program authorized the government purchase of up to $700 billion in toxic assets from the balance sheets of dozens of financial institutions. In December of 2008 the auto industry was also struggling because high gas prices and the difficulty their buyers had obtaining auto loans, which resulted in plummeting sales of SUVs and larger vehicles. The government's response was to allow Chrysler and General Motors access to TARP funds to help them stay solvent. The two automakers ended up drawing roughly $17 billion from TARP to stay afloat.

In response to the uncertainty of the economy, Utah State University (USU Partners in Business) presented a financial seminar titled, *Weathering the Financial Storm* on January 22, 2009. Their program cover page claimed, "This year's seminar focuses on the current state of the economy and prevailing financial trends,) My wife, who worked for Partners in Business at the time, had arranged for me to attend the seminar, with her usual instructions that I was to sit quietly and keep my mouth shut!

So, I dutifully sat on the very last row of the auditorium and waited patiently for the first keynote speaker, Frank Nothaft, Vice President and Chief Economist for Freddie Mac. He would be presenting a *Housing and Mortgage Update,* and his biographical information stated, *"Local house-price bubbles, rapid growth in non-traditional mortgage lending, and excess global liquidity are some of the factors that contributed to the financial market distress of 2008. Frank will discuss the recent trends in the housing and mortgage markets, locally and nationally, and what the outlook is for 2009. Frank is a widely quoted expert on housing and economic issues. He is responsible for primary and secondary mortgage market analysis and research, as well as macroeconomic analysis and forecasting. Previously, Frank was an economist with the Board of Governors of the Federal Reserve System,"* This I had to see, finally someone in the know was going to explain the appalling financial mess that the country was in, and I was ready to listen.

Mr. Nothaft began his presentation discussing the effects of the local housing bubbles that had created due to rapidly rising property values, and the access to easy, affordable, financing. He skimmed over the rapid growth in non-traditional mortgage lending products and the effect that excess global liquidity (irrational exuberance) had in the marketplace. But what was most surprising to me was his projection of the home-ownership rate from 1940 to 2008 on the video screen for everyone to see. (I have spend countless hours searching for that image from 2009 to this day, and the one provided below just cannot do justice to the one he showed to us that day. I was surprised at the steep incline in his chart, which looked to rise rapidly without any sign of a down turn over the years.) Then he told the audience, *"Given the data, we couldn't see this thing coming."*

This following chart is the most similar that I can find to his, but it doesn't even come close to the one Mr. Nothaft showed us. The decline in the late eighties shown above appeared as an insignificant tick in a steady incline until peaking out after 2000. I was shocked and almost fell out of my chair as this thought raced through my mind, *"What do you mean you couldn't see this economic downturn coming? You are supposed to be the economist, are you really telling us that this chart was the only one you ever looked at?"*

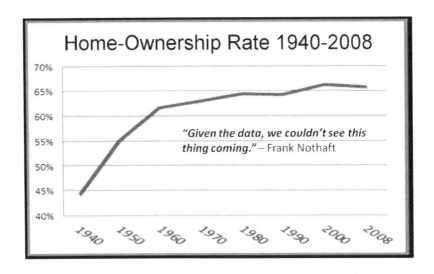

Home-Ownership Rate 1940-2008

"Given the data, we couldn't see this thing coming." – Frank Nothaft

But then, Mr. Nothaft dropped the big one! With an absolute straight face, he confidently declared, *"The recession will be over in six months!"* The puzzled reaction of the entire auditorium was shocked silence, and I could tell that everyone was anxiously waiting for Nothaft's presentation to be opened up to questions and answers. Our opportunity to question or challenge the ridiculous statements given to us quickly fizzled as the Master of Ceremonies, Tyler Bowles (Professor and Department Head of Economics and Finance,) stepped on to the stage singing praises to Mr. Nothaft and ushering him quickly off the stage, as his escorts whisked him to his waiting limousine to return him to the Salt Lake International airport for his flight back to Washington DC.

Mr. Bowles nervously faced the audience. He knew that we had not bought into Nothaft's message, and I was confident he knew that many of us were left wondering if this whole presentation had been a set up to spread political propaganda.

The audience was made up of students and local professionals, most of whom had paid a pretty significant fee for the privilege of attending this particular financial seminar. Bowles knew he had a problem on his hands. Nothaft's opening message was a disaster and the validity of their entire seminar was hanging in the balance. Hemming and hawing, Bowles finally said, *"Well, we think he (meaning Nothaft) is a little optimistic"* and he then began to introduce the next participants on the program. This was going to be interesting to watch, especially in the shadow of what we had just been presented, and they now had my full attention.

Next up was a panel discussion with the *Jon M. Huntsman School of Business Professors* who would be discussing *"The Financial Crisis: What Went Wrong?"* The panel was comprised of, the masters of ceremonies, Mr. Bowles, Frank Caliendo (Executive Director, Graduate Programs,) Jeffrey Doyle (George S. Eccles Chair Capital Markets Research, Associate Professor, Accountancy,) and Paul Fjeldsted (Finance Lecturer, & Former Managing Director of Citi Group Global Markets Inc.,) each of whom was now seated, at a row of tables, at the front and center of the stage.

The program information stated, *"This discussion will take us to the very heart of the current financial crisis. It will answer the following questions: What is the source of this crisis? Why did the government do what it did? What are the consequences of the bailout? Where do we go from here?"* Each participant took about 15 to 20 minutes to discuss their opinions and observations, from their respective experiences, about what had happened in the economy. At the end of their presentations, the audience was then given a chance to ask specific questions that the panel responded to.

I had kept my promise, even though I had been biting my lips, I kept my mouth shut! It had become blatantly obvious to me that every time someone would ask a pertinent question as to what we could do in moving forward in this *"new economy,"* everyone of the panel members seemed to dodge the audience's questions. I was becoming incensed by their avoidance because, after all, they were the ones who had indicated that they were going to be discussing *"Where do we go from here?"*

I couldn't take any more of this avoidance, and it was time to address the truth, so I stood up and raised my hand. After all, I didn't want to be missed sitting there all the way up on the back row. When I was called upon to ask my question, I spoke as loudly as I could, so no one would miss my question. I said, *"I have a question, but before I ask it I need to give a little background so you will understand my question. For the last 30 years, I have been involved in real estate, business and community development. I want to go back and discuss the previous speaker's presentation and the chart that he showed to us. If you recall, he said that because of the significant steady increase of home ownership that they could not see this housing crisis coming. But if you remember from his chart, there was a little tiny blip that occurred around 1988 to 1989. Some of you may remember, it was called the Saving and Loan Debacle. I was a real estate appraiser in Washington State until I retired in 2006. As a result of the economic problems associated with the Savings and Loan Debacle, the government acted to implement new regulations and programs like FIRREA and RESPA and others to protect us and guarantee that THIS WOULD NEVER HAPPEN AGAIN!"*

The auditorium was silent and you could have heard a pin drop. Every eye was looking in my direction, especially those who were sitting on the panel. I continued, *"I remember it well, because it turned my industry completely upside down. What you may not know is that when they implemented these new rules that were going to protect us, there was a $50,000 de minims clause that said any federally backed mortgage loan within the $50,000 threshold did not have to meet the new requirements that had been implemented to protect us. What you also may not know is that in 1996 President Bill Clinton raised the de minims amount to $250,000, which then allowed almost 80% of all mortgage loans to* *no longer be required to meet the requirements of the rules that had been implemented to protect us. But you are also probably not aware at the same time, President Bill Clinton implemented his Home Affordable program which mandated the used of "special affordable" loans, many of which did not require sufficient documentation of income, credit or property values, and it was these 'Liar Loans' as the industry called them, that have been blamed as the cause of the mortgage melt-down. However, what you probably don't know either is that banks who refused to offer the use of these 'special affordable' loans were penalized and threatened with the closure of their business if they would not comply. Now it is with this background and understanding that I ask my question,"* Anticipation and dread hung in the air waiting for me to speak again. Looking straight at the panel, I asked, *"WHAT MAKES YOU THINK THEY ARE GOING TO GET IT RIGHT THIS TIME?"*

I then sat back down. The effects of my question were immediate and it seemed like I had just detonated an emotional bomb. I felt bad that my question had just destroyed their conference, but what I had asked was on the heart of everyone present. Audible gasps could be heard as the audience began facing back toward the stage, where poor Mr. Bowles stood nervously stammering as he searched for something, anything, to say in response to my question.

Turning to his right, he faced the second member of the panel, Mr. Caliendo, and asked, *"How would you answer his question?"* Mr. Caliendo stutteringly replied, *"I, I, I didn't hear his question."* He then turned to face the third member of the panel and asked, *"How would you answer?"* Mr. Doyle hung his head and said, *"I don't know how to answer that."* He then turned to the last member of the panel, Mr. Fjeldsted and asked him, *"How would you answer his question?"* Mr. Fjeldsted was the newest member of the economics faculty having recently come from Wall Street where it was his job, as an analyst, to evaluate and value the Credit Default Swaps, which lay at the heart of our economic melt-down. Mr. Fjeldsted looked straight at me and then said, *"I don't know what to say other than he is right."* He then looked back to Mr. Bowles who was pacing and stammering looking for something to say. He paused and then smirkingly said, *"I didn't realize that we had Ron Paul[1] here with us today."* He then dismissed the session and they left the stage.

Volumes had been spoken and truths had been revealed, and for many in attendance that day, dirty little secrets had been let out of the bag.

[1]Ron Paul is an outspoken former member of the U.S. House of Representatives and three-time presidential candidate, who has tirelessly worked for limited, constitutional government, low taxes, free markets, and a return to sound monetary policies. He is noted for never voting for any legislation unless the proposed measure was expressly authorized by the Constitution.

Connections Between: Bundy Mistrial, Podesta Emails, & National Monuments
As told by Main Stream Media

The Washington Times reported on December 21, 2017 in an article titled, AG Sessions orders examination of Bundy case after mistrial over prosecution bungling: "Attorney General Jeff Sessions has stepped into the Bundy prosecution after Wednesday's mistrial, ordering a third-party examination of the case in light of the latest government snafu.

"The Attorney General takes this issue very seriously and has personally directed that an expert in the Department's discovery obligations be deployed to examine the case and advise as to the next steps," said Ian D. Prior, principal deputy director of public affairs, in a late Wednesday statement.

"The decision to intervene came after U.S. District Chief Judge Gloria Navarro declared a mistrial over the government's "willful failure to disclose information" to the defense, saying it would have been "impossible" for the four co-defendants to receive a fair trial.

"Failure to turn over such evidence violates due process," Chief Judge Navarro said in the courtroom as reported by the Arizona Republic. "A fair trial at this point is impossible."

"Nevada rancher Cliven Bundy, his sons Ammon and Ryan Bundy, and Ryan Payne of Montana have been charged with 15 felony counts stemming from the 2014 armed standoff with the Bureau of Land Management at the Bundy ranch near Bunkerville.

"The examination represents the first direct public intervention by the attorney general in the Nevada case, which began last year under then-Attorney General Loretta E. Lynch.

"Acting U.S. Attorney Steven W. Myhre, who oversees the prosecution, said he welcomed the input from Washington, D.C.

"We respect the ruling of the Court and take very seriously our discovery obligations," Mr. Myhre said in a statement. "The Office welcomes the assistance of the Attorney General as we continue to evaluate the case in light of the Court's ruling.

"No deadline was given for the attorney general's examination, but Chief Judge Navarro set a Jan. 8 hearing on defense motions to dismiss the case. The next trial is tentatively scheduled to begin Feb. 26.

"Mr. Sessions has said little in public about the Bundy case. One exception came during a July 12 speech to law enforcement in Las Vegas at which he praised Mr. Myhre and insisted, "I'm not taking sides or commenting on the case," according to the Las Vegas Review-Journal.

"The trial, which involves 19 defendants spread over three tiers, has been riddled with setbacks for the prosecution, including a previous mistrial, hung juries and acquittals on lesser figures in the April 2014 armed confrontation with BLM agents.

"Judge Navarro said the prosecutors had willfully failed to disclose key evidence in the case, including FBI records about surveillance and government snipers at the Bundy ranch; activity logs, law-enforcement threat assessments showing the Bundy family posed no threat of violence, and internal reports about BLM agent misconduct.

"She dismissed the jury after seven weeks in the latest trial involving the second of the three tiers of co-defendants.

"All four in the latest trial are considered leaders of the confrontation with the BLM, which began after agents tried to impound the ranch's cattle following Cliven Bundy's refusal for years to pay grazing fees in a protest over federal land management.

"Ian Bartrum, professor at the University of Nevada Las Vegas law school, said that some have questioned the Trump administration's commitment to the Bundy prosecution, given that "the Bundys are very popular among the Trump base,)

"I've even seen some [I think unfounded] claims that US Attorney's office has deliberately sabotaged its own prosecution," Mr. Bartrum said in an email. "I think that is very, very unlikely — but this could be a signal that the DOJ is taking the case very seriously, in order to quell those sorts of doubters,)

"On the other hand, he said, "this could foreshadow a way out for the prosecution,)

"In other words, the DOJ expert could come in, review the necessary disclosures, and conclude that the government can't win if it turns everything over," Mr. Bartrum said. "That would give the US Attorney cover to dismiss the case."

"The government lost its star witness earlier this year when Daniel Love, the BLM agent in charge of the Bundy operation, was fired after a federal investigation found that he misappropriated rare minerals and then told a subordinate to conceal the misconduct.

"He had previously been faulted for using his position to obtain tickets to the Burning Man festival.

"Larry Klayman, an attorney for Cliven Bundy, urged Mr. Sessions in a Thursday letter to order prosecutors to drop the charges and launch an ethics investigation against Mr. Myhre, his staff and "complicit FBI agents."

"Jeff, in the interests of justice, much less fundamental fairness, it is now incumbent that you do your job," said Mr. Klayman, founder of Judicial Watch and Freedom Watch. "To put it bluntly, the time has come to 'take sides.' This travesty must end now."

[The foregoing Washington Times article is located at: https://www.washingtontimes.com/news/2017/dec/21/jeff-sessions-orders-examination-bundy-case]

Protection or Profit?

An article by the Chicago Tribune on November 1, 2016 titled, In the Nevada desert, Bundy family warns of another standoff, states: "Less than a week after being acquitted for his role in last winter's armed occupation of an Oregon federal wildlife refuge, Nevada rancher Ryan Bundy said another protest action will be justified if President Barack Obama goes ahead with plans to create a huge national monument abutting the Bundy family's ranch here.

"Absolutely! That's the best thing in the world for [people] to do," Bundy said Monday in a telephone interview from an Oregon jail, where he is being held pending a February trial related to a separate armed standoff in 2014 with federal agents at his family's ranch.

"Read the Declaration of Independence," he said. "It says right there that if the government becomes abusive, it's our right and our duty to abolish that government. If the government won't restrain itself, whatever happens is their own fault."

"The suggestion of a potential uprising underscores the extent to which two competing political movements - defiance of federal authority, and Obama's determination to permanently protect vast federal lands - could collide next in this arid patch of land 110 miles northeast of Las Vegas.

"Federal officials were alarmed by the jury's decision to acquit Bundy, his brother Ammon and five others who staged a 41-day occupation early this year at the Malheur National Wildlife Refuge in remote eastern Oregon.

"While supporters of the Bundys hailed the surprise verdict as a victory against what they see as federal overreach, federal officials said it could embolden anyone with a grievance to take over government property and endanger federal workers.

"Ryan Bundy is angry that Obama, before he leaves office, may use his executive power under the 1906 Antiquities Act to impose new restrictions on Gold Butte, a 350,000-acre parcel of pristine desert wilderness just south of the Bundy family's ranch.

"Obama administration officials said federal officials were rattled by the Oregon verdict, but individuals briefed on the process say the White House is pushing ahead with plans to create a monument that would permanently preserve a federally owned tract filled with soaring peaks, exotic red sandstone formations, an imperiled desert tortoise population and thousands of ancient Native American rock etchings called petroglyphs.

"Senate Minority Leader Harry Reid, D-Nevada, who has worked to protect the area for years, has described a monument designation as one of his final goals before retiring this year.

"Bundy, 44, wouldn't say whether he and his family would encourage some kind of anti-government action over Gold Butte, because "I never say what we will do." But asked whether violence was ever justified against an abusive government, Bundy said: "Ask George Washington."

"Repeating an argument common in the West but disputed by most mainstream constitutional scholars, Bundy said the Constitution does not grant the federal government power to own large tracts of land, nor does the president have legal authority to create national monuments. Bundy said that creating the Gold Butte monument would be an abuse of presidential power and a valuation of tourism and endangered species over the economic needs of struggling communities.

"The government should be scared. They are in the wrong. The land does not belong to the government. The land belongs to the people of Clark County, not to the people of the United States," said Bundy, who spoke over the phone as his wife, Angie, sat nearby beneath a shady mesquite tree at the family's 160-acre ranch on the parched banks of the Virgin River.

"The only peaceful resolution to all this is for them to obey the Constitution," he said. "Read it, understand it, abide by it. There doesn't have to be violence. None of that has to happen if they would just abide by the Constitution."

"That kind of talk is exactly what officials have worried about after the Oregon verdict. They fear that a potential flash point for anti-government action could be Obama's fast-paced creation of national monuments where grazing, timber-cutting, mining and other commercial activities are generally prohibited. Obama has already created or expanded 27 national monuments, more than any other president since Franklin D. Roosevelt.

"For many generations, ranchers in Bunkerville have paid a fee to graze their cattle on the Gold Butte land, but nearly all of them allowed the Nature Conservancy and other groups to buy out their permits years ago. The Bundy family, which has fewer than 600 head of cattle, is the last full-time ranching family in the area. Their animals still graze for free, as they have for years, in defiance of federal courts twice ordering the Bundys to desist. The family has refused to pay more than $1 million in fees and fines.

"When officials from the Bureau of Land Management (BLM) and the National Park Service tried to finally remove the cattle in 2014, they were met by the Bundy family and hundreds of armed supporters.

"Fearing bloodshed, authorities eventually retreated. Earlier this year, family patriarch Cliven Bundy, along with sons Ammon and Ryan, and 16 others, were charged with an array of federal firearms, conspiracy and assault counts in the 2014 incident. They face trial in Nevada in February.

"Interior Secretary Sally Jewell has called the Nevada standoff the worst moment of her tenure. And after last week's acquittal in Oregon, she warned her employees, including those at the BLM, to "take care of yourselves" and "remain vigilant."

A coalition of environmentalists, tribal groups, academics and some business owners eagerly support the Gold Butte plan.

"Gold Butte has captivating landscapes that Americans across the country would love to explore," Sierra Club Executive Director Michael Brune said in an interview. "But it's also home to thousands of archaeological sites that currently have no protection and that could be enjoyed and studied for future generations."

"Reid has been the highest-profile advocate for the project. He has devoted much of his career to brokering such deals: During his 34 years in Congress, the amount of federal land off limits to development in Nevada has grown from 67,000 acres to 4.8 million acres.

"Speaking on the Senate floor just after Bundys were arrested this year, Reid said: "I've tried to protect Gold Butte for a long time. And the reason we haven't been able to do anything to this point is the Bundy boys and their pals. So that's why I'm grateful for the Antiquities Act. Because of this legislation and because of the fact that the Bundys are in jail, I'm going to reach out to the White House."

"As he has lobbied the administration, Reid has framed the issue as a test of federal will. "Let's tell others how important this is," he said during a news conference in August, "and tell people to keep their damn hands off public lands."

"Republicans have opposed Obama's use of "unilateral" executive power to create national monuments. "The establishment of any new national monument in the State of Nevada, regardless of location, ought to be considered in the public Congressional process," Sen. Dean Heller, R-Nevada, wrote in an April letter to the president.

"On the Bundy ranch, Angie Bundy said that "Harry Reid has no right to be saying those things." She said she suspects that the federal government is trying to claim more land to keep control of uranium and other minerals. She said federal officials should respect local ranchers more and recognize that they are far more effective stewards of the land than "bureaucrats from back East."

"They should let people who have been protecting this land for generations take care of it," she said. "And they shouldn't be sending in heavily armed military forces to point weapons at a rancher who hasn't paid his taxes."

"On Monday, Reid said in a statement that the Gold Butte monument would not be derailed by threats of resistance from "radicals . . . intent on using public lands like Gold Butte for their own selfish purposes."

"That kind of talk infuriates Duane Magoon, a rancher and Bunkerville town official who was raised by the Bundy family. He said he doubted that local people would rise up against the government over Gold Butte, as they did in Oregon or at the Bundy ranch in 2014. But, he said, "you never know."

"Why would the feds even want to find out? Is the government stupid?" he said. "They are aware that we are upset. Why would they rock that boat? If something happens, it's because of them."

"Deep in the heart of Gold Butte one hot afternoon this week, Jim Boone hiked among the otherworldly swirling and jagged sandstone formations known as Little Finland. He admired petroglyphs carved into black stone and salt formations that turned the rock a vibrant shade of blue.

"Boone, an ecologist and writer who chronicles Gold Butte's wildlife and history, said lush vegetation covered this area thousands of years ago. But over the centuries, the land has dried out, and today the vegetation is mainly prickly brush and creosote bushes.

"Not far from the Bundy ranch, Boone pulled off the gravel road to look at about 20 of the family's cattle grazing on the parched land.

"In a way, you can understand the Bundys," he said. "The world is changing all around them, the environment and the politics, and all they want to do is have the world stay the same and let their grandchildren do exactly what they did."

[The foregoing Chicago Tribune article is located at: http://www.chicagotribune.com/news/nationworld/ct-bundy-family-standoff-20161101-story.html]

Solar or Nuclear Energy?

Almost everyone is familiar with the Bundy Ranch standoff with the Bureau Of Land Management. It was a 20 year legal dispute between the government and a cattle rancher by the name of Cliven Bundy, which ended with Bundy's supporters gathering on his land, armed with rifles, and pushing back police and other authorities until they finally gave up.

The BLM had managed to gain court orders against Bundy, ordering him to pay over a million dollars in withheld grazing fees for his use of the federally owned land which was next to his ranch. Bundy was eventually banned from grazing his cattle on government land. In another case surrounding the Hammond Ranch, the owners had inadvertently set fire to government land while performing a controlled burn on their own property. The federal government decided to make an example of the Hammond family, charging them with crimes of terrorism.

We were told in various news reports that Harry Reid, former U.S. Senator from Nevada, had his eyes on the Bundy Ranch for the future sight of a solar farm involving Chinese corporations, and of course his involvement would make him a lot of money for his participation.

A Reuters article dated August 30, 2012 stated, "*The Langfang, China-based ENN Energy Group hopes to build what would be the largest solar energy complex in America. The site chosen with (Harry's son) Rory Reid's guidance is in tiny Laughlin, Nevada, a gambling town of 7,300 along the Colorado River, 90 miles south of Las Vegas,)*

So, how exactly does a designation of a national monument work for building a solar farm? Maybe we misunderstood Harry Reid when he said solar energy, maybe he actually meant nuclear energy, like uranium! Uranium is the prime ingredient in nuclear energy. It is used around the world to produce electricity and other powerful devises, and it is in high demand. One location in the United States where uranium is usually located, is southeastern Nevada, and it just so happens that the Bundy Ranch is also be located in southeastern Nevada. Could this be the real reason our government has been after the Bundy Ranch?

The Connecting Email Scandal

The Clinton-Podesta email scandal is full of references to both pedophilila and satanism, such as "spirit cooking" and "sacrificing a chicken ... to Moloch" (email #30489 via WikiLeaks,) which are disturbing enough, but According to WikiLeaks founder Julian Assange, the emails — which are labeled as "Part I of the Podesta emails" — focus on Podesta's "communications relating to nuclear energy, and media handling over donations to the Clinton Foundation from mining and nuclear interests." (TheHill.Com) - This is a much bigger story than most realize.

On April 23, 2015 a New York Times article titled, Cash Flowed to Clinton Foundation Amid Russian Uranium Deal stated: "The headline on the website Pravda trumpeted President Vladimir V. Putin's latest coup, its nationalistic fervor recalling an era when its precursor served as the official mouthpiece of the Kremlin: "Russian Nuclear Energy Conquers the World."

"The article, in January 2013, detailed how the Russian atomic energy agency, Rosatom, had taken over a Canadian company with uranium-mining stakes stretching from Central Asia to the American West. The deal made Rosatom one of the world's largest uranium producers and brought Mr. Putin closer to his goal of controlling much of the global uranium supply chain.

"But the untold story behind that story is one that involves not just the Russian president, but also a former American president and a woman who would like to be the next one.

"At the heart of the tale are several men, leaders of the Canadian mining industry, who have been major donors to the charitable endeavors of former President Bill Clinton and his family. Members of that group built, financed and eventually sold off to the Russians a company that would become known as Uranium One.

"Beyond mines in Kazakhstan that are among the most lucrative in the world, the sale gave the Russians control of one-fifth of all uranium production capacity in the United States. Since uranium is considered a strategic asset, with implications for national security, the deal had to be approved by a committee composed of representatives from a number of United States government agencies. Among the agencies that eventually signed off was the State Department, then headed by Mr. Clinton's wife, Hillary Rodham Clinton.

"As the Russians gradually assumed control of Uranium One in three separate transactions from 2009 to 2013, Canadian records show, a flow of cash made its way to the Clinton Foundation. Uranium One's chairman used his family foundation to make four donations totaling $2.35 million. Those contributions were not publicly disclosed by the Clintons, despite an agreement Mrs. Clinton had struck with the Obama White House to publicly identify all donors. Other people with ties to the company made donations as well.

"And shortly after the Russians announced their intention to acquire a majority stake in Uranium One, Mr. Clinton received $500,000 for a Moscow speech from a Russian investment bank with links to the Kremlin that was promoting Uranium One stock.

"At the time, both Rosatom and the United States government made promises intended to ease concerns about ceding control of the company's assets to the Russians. Those promises have been repeatedly broken, records show.

"The New York Times's examination of the Uranium One deal is based on dozens of interviews, as well as a review of public records and securities filings in Canada, Russia and the United States. Some of the connections between Uranium One and the Clinton Foundation were unearthed by Peter Schweizer, a former fellow at the right-leaning Hoover Institution and author of the forthcoming book "Clinton Cash,) Mr. Schweizer provided a preview of material in the book to The Times, which scrutinized his information and built upon it with its own reporting.

"Whether the donations played any role in the approval of the uranium deal is unknown. But the episode underscores the special ethical challenges presented by the Clinton Foundation, headed by a former president who relied heavily on foreign cash to accumulate $250 million in assets even as his wife helped steer American foreign policy as secretary of state, presiding over decisions with the potential to benefit the foundation's donors.

"In a statement, Brian Fallon, a spokesman for Mrs. Clinton's presidential campaign, said no one "has ever produced a shred of evidence supporting the theory that Hillary Clinton ever took action as secretary of state to support the interests of donors to the Clinton Foundation,) He emphasized that multiple United States agencies, as well as the Canadian government, had signed off on the deal and that, in general, such matters were handled at a level below the secretary. "To suggest the State Department, under then-Secretary Clinton, exerted undue influence in the U.S. government's review of the sale of Uranium One is utterly baseless," he added.

"American political campaigns are barred from accepting foreign donations. But foreigners may give to foundations in the United States. In the days since Mrs. Clinton announced her candidacy for president, the Clinton Foundation has announced changes meant to quell longstanding concerns about potential conflicts of interest in such donations; it has limited donations from foreign governments, with many, like Russia's, barred from giving to all but its health care initiatives. That policy stops short of a more stringent agreement between Mrs. Clinton and the Obama administration that was in effect while she was secretary of state.

"Either way, the Uranium One deal highlights the limits of such prohibitions. The foundation will continue to accept contributions from foreign sources whose interests, like Uranium One's, may overlap with those of foreign governments, some of which may be at odds with the United States.

"When the Uranium One deal was approved, the geopolitical backdrop was far different from today's. The Obama administration was seeking to "reset" strained relations with Russia. The deal was strategically important to Mr. Putin, who shortly after the Americans gave their blessing sat down for a staged interview with Rosatom's chief executive, Sergei Kiriyenko. "Few could have imagined in the past that we would own 20 percent of U.S. reserves," Mr. Kiriyenko told Mr. Putin.

"Now, after Russia's annexation of Crimea and aggression in Ukraine, the Moscow-Washington relationship is devolving toward Cold War levels, a point several experts made in evaluating a deal so beneficial to Mr. Putin, a man known to use energy resources to project power around the world.

"Should we be concerned? Absolutely," said Michael McFaul, who served under Mrs. Clinton as the American ambassador to Russia but said he had been unaware of the Uranium One deal until asked about it. "Do we want Putin to have a monopoly on this? Of course we don't. We don't want to be dependent on Putin for anything in this climate."

"A Seat at the Table - The path to a Russian acquisition of American uranium deposits began in 2005 in Kazakhstan, where the Canadian mining financier Frank Giustra orchestrated his first big uranium deal, with Mr. Clinton at his side.

"The two men had flown aboard Mr. Giustra's private jet to Almaty, Kazakhstan, where they dined with the authoritarian president, Nursultan A. Nazarbayev. Mr. Clinton handed the Kazakh president a propaganda coup when he expressed support for Mr. Nazarbayev's bid to head an international elections monitoring group, undercutting American foreign policy and criticism of Kazakhstan's poor human rights record by, among others, his wife, then a senator.

"Within days of the visit, Mr. Giustra's fledgling company, UrAsia Energy Ltd., signed a preliminary deal giving it stakes in three uranium mines controlled by the state-run uranium agency Kazatomprom.

"If the Kazakh deal was a major victory, UrAsia did not wait long before resuming the hunt. In 2007, it merged with Uranium One, a South African company with assets in Africa and Australia, in what was described as a $3.5 billion transaction. The new company, which kept the Uranium One name, was controlled by UrAsia investors including Ian Telfer, a Canadian who became chairman. Through a spokeswoman, Mr. Giustra, whose personal stake in the deal was estimated at about $45 million, said he sold his stake in 2007.

"Soon, Uranium One began to snap up companies with assets in the United States. In April 2007, it announced the purchase of a uranium mill in Utah and more than 38,000 acres of uranium exploration properties in four Western states, followed quickly by the acquisition of the Energy Metals Corporation and its uranium holdings in Wyoming, Texas and Utah. That deal made clear that Uranium One was intent on becoming "a powerhouse in the United States uranium sector with the potential to become the domestic supplier of choice for U.S. utilities," the company declared.

"Still, the company's story was hardly front-page news in the United States — until early 2008, in the midst of Mrs. Clinton's failed presidential campaign, when The Times published an article revealing the 2005 trip's link to Mr. Giustra's Kazakhstan mining deal. It also reported that several months later, Mr. Giustra had donated $31.3 million to Mr. Clinton's foundation.

"(In a statement issued after this article appeared online, Mr. Giustra said he was "extremely proud" of his charitable work with Mr. Clinton, and he urged the media to focus on poverty, health care and "the real challenges of the world."

"Though the 2008 article quoted the former head of Kazatomprom, Moukhtar Dzhakishev, as saying that the deal required government approval and was discussed at a dinner with the president, Mr. Giustra insisted that it was a private transaction, with no need for Mr. Clinton's influence with Kazakh officials. He described his relationship with Mr. Clinton as motivated solely by a shared interest in philanthropy.

"As if to underscore the point, five months later Mr. Giustra held a fund-raiser for the Clinton Giustra Sustainable Growth Initiative, a project aimed at fostering progressive environmental and labor practices in the natural resources industry, to which he had pledged $100 million. The star-studded gala, at a conference center in Toronto, featured performances by Elton John and Shakira and celebrities like Tom Cruise, John Travolta and Robin Williams encouraging contributions from the many so-called F.O.F.s — Friends of Frank — in attendance, among them Mr. Telfer. In all, the evening generated $16 million in pledges, according to an article in The Globe and Mail.

"None of this would have been possible if Frank Giustra didn't have a remarkable combination of caring and modesty, of vision and energy and iron determination," Mr. Clinton told those gathered, adding: "I love this guy, and you should, too."

"But what had been a string of successes was about to hit a speed bump.

"Arrest and Progress - By June 2009, a little over a year after the star-studded evening in Toronto, Uranium One's stock was in free-fall, down 40 percent. Mr. Dzhakishev, the head of Kazatomprom, had just been arrested on charges that he illegally sold uranium deposits to foreign companies, including at least some of those won by Mr. Giustra's UrAsia and now owned by Uranium One.

"Publicly, the company tried to reassure shareholders. Its chief executive, Jean Nortier, issued a confident statement calling the situation a "complete misunderstanding,) He also contradicted Mr. Giustra's contention that the uranium deal had not required government blessing. "When you do a transaction in Kazakhstan, you need the government's approval," he said, adding that UrAsia had indeed received that approval.

"But privately, Uranium One officials were worried they could lose their joint mining ventures. American diplomatic cables made public by WikiLeaks also reflect concerns that Mr. Dzhakishev's arrest was part of a Russian power play for control of Kazakh uranium assets.

"At the time, Russia was already eying a stake in Uranium One, Rosatom company documents show. Rosatom officials say they were seeking to acquire mines around the world because Russia lacks sufficient domestic reserves to meet its own industry needs.

"It was against this backdrop that the Vancouver-based Uranium One pressed the American Embassy in Kazakhstan, as well as Canadian diplomats, to take up its cause with Kazakh officials, according to the American cables.

"We want more than a statement to the press," Paul Clarke, a Uranium One executive vice president, told the embassy's energy officer on June 10, the officer reported in a cable. "That is simply chitchat,) What the company needed, Mr. Clarke said, was official written confirmation that the licenses were valid.

"The American Embassy ultimately reported to the secretary of state, Mrs. Clinton. Though the Clarke cable was copied to her, it was given wide circulation, and it is unclear if she would have read it; the Clinton campaign did not address questions about the cable.

"What is clear is that the embassy acted, with the cables showing that the energy officer met with Kazakh officials to discuss the issue on June 10 and 11.

"Three days later, a wholly owned subsidiary of Rosatom completed a deal for 17 percent of Uranium One. And within a year, the Russian government substantially upped the ante, with a generous offer to shareholders that would give it a 51 percent controlling stake. But first, Uranium One had to get the American government to sign off on the deal.

"When a company controlled by the Chinese government sought a 51 percent stake in a tiny Nevada gold mining operation in 2009, it set off a secretive review process in Washington, where officials raised concerns primarily about the mine's proximity to a military installation, but also about the potential for minerals at the site, including uranium, to come under Chinese control. The officials killed the deal.

"Such is the power of the Committee on Foreign Investment in the United States. The committee comprises some of the most powerful members of the cabinet, including the attorney general, the secretaries of the Treasury, Defense, Homeland Security, Commerce and Energy, and the secretary of state. They are charged with reviewing any deal that could result in foreign control of an American business or asset deemed important to national security.

"The national security issue at stake in the Uranium One deal was not primarily about nuclear weapons proliferation; the United States and Russia had for years cooperated on that front, with Russia sending enriched fuel from decommissioned warheads to be used in American nuclear power plants in return for raw uranium.

"Instead, it concerned American dependence on foreign uranium sources. While the United States gets one-fifth of its electrical power from nuclear plants, it produces only around 20 percent of the uranium it needs, and most plants have only 18 to 36 months of reserves, according to Marin Katusa, author of "The Colder War: How the Global Energy Trade Slipped From America's Grasp."

"The Russians are easily winning the uranium war, and nobody's talking about it," said Mr. Katusa, who explores the implications of the Uranium One deal in his book. "It's not just a domestic issue but a foreign policy issue, too."

"When ARMZ, an arm of Rosatom, took its first 17 percent stake in Uranium One in 2009, the two parties signed an agreement, found in securities filings, to seek the foreign investment committee's review. But it was the 2010 deal, giving the Russians a controlling 51 percent stake, that set off alarm bells. Four members of the House of Representatives signed a letter expressing concern. Two more began pushing legislation to kill the deal.

"Senator John Barrasso, a Republican from Wyoming, where Uranium One's largest American operation was, wrote to President Obama, saying the deal "would give the Russian government control over a sizable portion of America's uranium production capacity."

"Equally alarming," Mr. Barrasso added, "this sale gives ARMZ a significant stake in uranium mines in Kazakhstan."

"Uranium One's shareholders were also alarmed, and were "afraid of Rosatom as a Russian state giant," Sergei Novikov, a company spokesman, recalled in an interview. He said Rosatom's chief, Mr. Kiriyenko, sought to reassure Uranium One investors, promising that Rosatom would not break up the company and would keep the same management, including Mr. Telfer, the chairman. Another Rosatom official said publicly that it did not intend to increase its investment beyond 51 percent, and that it envisioned keeping Uranium One a public company

"American nuclear officials, too, seemed eager to assuage fears. The Nuclear Regulatory Commission wrote to Mr. Barrasso assuring him that American uranium would be preserved for domestic use, regardless of who owned it.

"In order to export uranium from the United States, Uranium One Inc. or ARMZ would need to apply for and obtain a specific NRC license authorizing the export of uranium for use as reactor fuel," the letter said.

"Still, the ultimate authority to approve or reject the Russian acquisition rested with the cabinet officials on the foreign investment committee, including Mrs. Clinton — whose husband was collecting millions in donations from people associated with Uranium One.

"Undisclosed Donations - Before Mrs. Clinton could assume her post as secretary of state, the White House demanded that she sign a memorandum of understanding placing limits on the activities of her husband's foundation. To avoid the perception of conflicts of interest, beyond the ban on foreign government donations, the foundation was required to publicly disclose all contributors.

"To judge from those disclosures — which list the contributions in ranges rather than precise amounts — the only Uranium One official to give to the Clinton Foundation was Mr. Telfer, the chairman, and the amount was relatively small: no more than $250,000, and that was in 2007, before talk of a Rosatom deal began percolating.

"But a review of tax records in Canada, where Mr. Telfer has a family charity called the Fernwood Foundation, shows that he donated millions of dollars more, during and after the critical time when the foreign investment committee was reviewing his deal with the Russians. With the Russians offering a special dividend, shareholders like Mr. Telfer stood to profit.

"His donations through the Fernwood Foundation included $1 million reported in 2009, the year his company appealed to the American Embassy to help it keep its mines in Kazakhstan; $250,000 in 2010, the year the Russians sought majority control; as well as $600,000 in 2011 and $500,000 in 2012. Mr. Telfer said that his donations had nothing to do with his business dealings, and that he had never discussed Uranium One with Mr. or Mrs.

Clinton. He said he had given the money because he wanted to support Mr. Giustra's charitable endeavors with Mr. Clinton. "Frank and I have been friends and business partners for almost 20 years," he said.

"The Clinton campaign left it to the foundation to reply to questions about the Fernwood donations; the foundation did not provide a response.

"Mr. Telfer's undisclosed donations came in addition to between $1.3 million and $5.6 million in contributions, which were reported, from a constellation of people with ties to Uranium One or UrAsia, the company that originally acquired Uranium One's most valuable asset: the Kazakh mines. Without those assets, the Russians would have had no interest in the deal: "It wasn't the goal to buy the Wyoming mines. The goal was to acquire the Kazakh assets, which are very good," Mr. Novikov, the Rosatom spokesman, said in an interview.

"Amid this influx of Uranium One-connected money, Mr. Clinton was invited to speak in Moscow in June 2010, the same month Rosatom struck its deal for a majority stake in Uranium One.

"The $500,000 fee — among Mr. Clinton's highest — was paid by Renaissance Capital, a Russian investment bank with ties to the Kremlin that has invited world leaders, including Tony Blair, the former British prime minister, to speak at its investor conferences.

"Renaissance Capital analysts talked up Uranium One's stock, assigning it a "buy" rating and saying in a July 2010 research report that it was "the best play" in the uranium markets. In addition, Renaissance Capital turned up that same year as a major donor, along with Mr. Giustra and several companies linked to Uranium One or UrAsia, to a small medical charity in Colorado run by a friend of Mr. Giustra's. In a newsletter to supporters, the friend credited Mr. Giustra with helping get donations from "businesses around the world."

"Renaissance Capital would not comment on the genesis of Mr.

Clinton's speech to an audience that included leading Russian officials, or on whether it was connected to the Rosatom deal. According to a Russian government news service, Mr. Putin personally thanked Mr. Clinton for speaking.

"A person with knowledge of the Clinton Foundation's fund-raising operation, who requested anonymity to speak candidly about it, said that for many people, the hope is that money will in fact buy influence: "Why do you think they are doing it — because they love them?" But whether it actually does is another question. And in this case, there were broader geopolitical pressures that likely came into play as the United States considered whether to approve the Rosatom-Uranium One deal.

"Diplomatic Considerations - "If doing business with Rosatom was good for those in the Uranium One deal, engaging with Russia was also a priority of the incoming Obama administration, which was hoping for a new era of cooperation as Mr. Putin relinquished the presidency — if only for a term — to Dmitri A. Medvedev.

"The assumption was we could engage Russia to further core U.S. national security interests," said Mr. McFaul, the former ambassador.

"It started out well. The two countries made progress on nuclear proliferation issues, and expanded use of Russian territory to resupply American forces in Afghanistan. Keeping Iran from obtaining a nuclear weapon was among the United States' top priorities, and in June 2010 Russia signed off on a United Nations resolution imposing tough new sanctions on that country.

"Two months later, the deal giving ARMZ a controlling stake in Uranium One was submitted to the Committee on Foreign Investment in the United States for review. Because of the secrecy surrounding the process, it is hard to know whether the participants weighed the desire to improve bilateral relations against the potential risks of allowing the Russian government control over the biggest uranium producer in the United States. The deal was ultimately approved in October, following what two people involved in securing the approval said had been a relatively smooth process.

"Not all of the committee's decisions are personally debated by the agency heads themselves; in less controversial cases, deputy or assistant secretaries may sign off. But experts and former committee members say Russia's interest in Uranium One and its American uranium reserves seemed to warrant attention at the highest levels.

"This deal had generated press, it had captured the attention of Congress and it was strategically important," said Richard Russell, who served on the committee during the George W. Bush administration. "When I was there invariably any one of those conditions would cause this to get pushed way up the chain, and here you had all three."

"And Mrs. Clinton brought a reputation for hawkishness to the process; as a senator, she was a vocal critic of the committee's approval of a deal that would have transferred the management of major American seaports to a company based in the United Arab Emirates, and as a presidential candidate she had advocated legislation to strengthen the process.

"The Clinton campaign spokesman, Mr. Fallon, said that in general, these matters did not rise to the secretary's level. He would not comment on whether Mrs. Clinton had been briefed on the matter, but he gave The Times a statement from the former assistant secretary assigned to the foreign investment committee at the time, Jose Fernandez. While not addressing the specifics of the Uranium One deal, Mr. Fernandez said, "Mrs. Clinton never intervened with me on any C.F.I.U.S. matter."

"Mr. Fallon also noted that if any agency had raised national security concerns about the Uranium One deal, it could have taken them directly to the president.

"Anne-Marie Slaughter, the State Department's director of policy planning at the time, said she was unaware of the transaction — or the extent to which it made Russia a dominant uranium supplier. But speaking generally, she urged caution in evaluating its wisdom in hindsight.

"Russia was not a country we took lightly at the time or thought was cuddly," she said. "But it wasn't the adversary it is today."

"That renewed adversarial relationship has raised concerns about European dependency on Russian energy resources, including nuclear fuel. The unease reaches beyond diplomatic circles. In Wyoming, where Uranium One equipment is scattered across his 35,000-acre ranch, John Christensen is frustrated that repeated changes in corporate ownership over the years led to French, South African, Canadian and, finally, Russian control over mining rights on his property.

"I hate to see a foreign government own mining rights here in the United States," he said. "I don't think that should happen."

"Mr. Christensen, 65, noted that despite assurances by the Nuclear Regulatory Commission that uranium could not leave the country without Uranium One or ARMZ obtaining an export license — which they do not have — yellowcake from his property was routinely packed into drums and trucked off to a processing plant in Canada.

"Asked about that, the commission confirmed that Uranium One has, in fact, shipped yellowcake to Canada even though it does not have an export license. Instead, the transport company doing the shipping, RSB Logistic Services, has the license. A commission spokesman said that "to the best of our knowledge" most of the uranium sent to Canada for processing was returned for use in the United States. A Uranium One spokeswoman, Donna Wichers, said 25 percent had gone to Western Europe and Japan. At the moment, with the uranium market in a downturn, nothing is being shipped from the Wyoming mines.

"The "no export" assurance given at the time of the Rosatom deal is not the only one that turned out to be less than it seemed.

Despite pledges to the contrary, Uranium One was delisted from the Toronto Stock Exchange and taken private. As of 2013, Rosatom's subsidiary, ARMZ, owned 100 percent of it.

"Correction: April 23, 2015 - An earlier version of this article misstated, in one instance, the surname of a fellow at the Hoover Institution. He is Peter Schweizer, not Schweitzer. An earlier version also incorrectly described the Clinton Foundation's agreement with the Obama administration regarding foreign-government donations while Hillary Rodham Clinton was secretary of state. Under the agreement, the foundation would not accept new donations from foreign governments, though it could seek State Department waivers in specific cases. It was not barred from accepting all foreign-government donations.

"Correction: April 30, 2015 - An article on Friday about contributions to the Clinton Foundation from people associated with a Canadian uranium-mining company described incorrectly the foundation's agreement with the Obama administration regarding foreign-government donations while Hillary Clinton was secretary of state. Under the agreement, the foundation would not accept new donations from foreign governments, though it could seek State Department waivers in specific cases. The foundation was not barred from accepting all foreign-government donations."

[The foregoing New York Times article is located at: https://www.nytimes.com/2015/04/24/us/cash-flowed-to-clinton-foundation-as-russians-pressed-for-control-of-uranium-company.html]

National Monument Land Grab

The Grand Staircase-Escalante National Monument is a U.S. national monument that originally designated 1,880,461 acres (7,610 km2) of protected land in southern Utah in 1996. The monument's size was later reduced by a succeeding presidential proclamation in 2017. The land is among the most remote in the country being the last to be mapped in the contiguous United States.

There are three main regions: the Grand Staircase, the Kaiparowits Plateau, and the Canyons of the Escalante(River). All regions are administered by the Bureau of Land Management (BLM) as part of the National Conservation Lands system. President Bill Clinton designated the area as a national monument in 1996 using his authority under the Antiquities Act. Grand Staircase-Escalante is the largest national monument managed by the BLM. The monument is managed by the Bureau of Land Management rather than the National Park Service. This was the first national monument managed by the BLM. Visitor centers are located in Cannonville, Big Water, Escalante, and Kanab.

The monument was declared on September 18, 1996 at the height of the 1996 presidential election campaign by President Bill Clinton, and was controversial from the moment of creation. The declaration ceremony was held at Grand Canyon National Park in Arizona, rather than in Utah. The Utah congressional delegation and state governor were notified only 24 hours before the ceremony. In the 1992 election, Clinton had placed third in the popular vote for the state of Utah, behind incumbent George H. W. Bush and independent candidate Ross Perot. In 1996, Clinton lost in Utah to Republican Bob Dole by a margin of 21.1%, but won in Arizona by 2.2%.

Local officials and Congressman Bill Orton (D - UT) objected to the designation of the monument, questioning whether the Antiquities Act allowed such vast amounts of land to be designated. However, United States Supreme Court decisions have long established the president's discretion to protect land under the Antiquities Act, and several lawsuits filed in an effort to overturn the designation were dismissed by federal courts. Monument designation also nixed the Andalex Coal Mine that was proposed for a remote location on the Kaiparowits Plateau.

Wilderness designation for the lands in the monument had long been sought by environmental groups; however, designation of the monument is not the same as wilderness designation, as activities such as motorized vehicle and mountain bike use are allowed.

There are contentious issues peculiar to the state of Utah. Certain plots of land were assigned when Utah became a state (in 1896) as School and Institutional Trust Lands (SITLa, a Utah state agency,) to be managed to produce funds for the state school system. These lands included scattered plots in the monument that could no longer be developed. The SITLa plots within the monument were exchanged for federal lands elsewhere in Utah, plus equivalent mineral rights and $50 million cash by an act of Congress, the Utah Schools and Lands Exchange Act of 1998, supported by Democrats and Republicans, and signed into law as Public Law 105-335 on October 31, 1998.

A more difficult problem is the resolution of United States Revised statute 2477 (R.S. 2477) road claims. R.S. 2477 (Section 8 of the 1866 Mining Act) states: "The right-of-way for the construction of highways over public lands, not reserved for public uses, is hereby granted,) The statute was repealed by the Federal Land Policy and Management Act (FLPMA) of 1976, but the repeal was subject to valid existing rights. A process for resolving disputed claims has not been established, and in 1996, the 104th Congress passed a law which prohibited Clinton-administration RS2477 proposed resolution regulations from taking effect without Congressional approval. The right to maintain and improve the many unpaved roads in the monument is disputed, with county officials placing county road signs on the roads they claim and occasionally applying bulldozers to grade claimed roads, while the BLM tries to exert control over the same roads. Litigation between the state and federal government over R.S. 2477 and road maintenance in the monument is an ongoing issue. (Wikipedia reference)

President Obama created Bears Ears National Monument on December 28, 2016 and on December 4, 2017 President Trump acted to gut the monument. The Bears Ears are two prominent buttes that rise high above Cedar Mesa in southeastern Utah. They are surrounded by a living cultural landscape of mountain peaks, verdant high plateaus, and roughhewn canyon country that is home to cliff dwellings, prehistoric villages, and rock art panels of ancestral Puebloan peoples. Located just south and east of

Canyonlands National Park, this landscape is significant to all Americans and indispensable to tribal peoples of the Colorado Plateau who rely on these sacred lands as a place of subsistence, spirituality, healing, and contemplation.

The Grand Canyon Trust was established in 1985 by Arizona Governor Bruce Babbitt and other leading conservationists (liberals) to work on natural resource issues affecting the Grand Canyon. Soon after, Executive Director Ed Norton and Trustee Stewart Udall made an impassioned plea: Since issues do not stop at the boundaries of Grand Canyon National Park, the Trust should be an advocate for both the Grand Canyon and the surrounding Colorado Plateau. The suggestion was adopted and the Grand Canyon Trust emerged as a leading regional conservation organization, with offices across the plateau and extensive connections among policymakers, land managers, scientists, and community leaders. Today, the trust employs a professional staff of 28, encompassing a wide range of skills from biology and forestry to economics and law. We have 23 committed trustees, a national membership of more than 3,500, and an active seasonal volunteer workforce of more than 400 people who assist with conservation projects.

Since 1985, the Grand Canyon Trust has worked diligently to protect the Grand Canyon and the Colorado Plateau. From banning uranium mining around the Grand Canyon to leading hundreds of volunteer projects, we're a leading voice for conservation of this spectacular place. From spearheading the removal of 16 million tons of uranium tailings poisoning the Colorado River near Moab, Utah, to negotiating the shut down the Mohave Generating Station (one of the largest sources of air pollution and carbon emissions on the Colorado Plateau,) since 1985 the Grand Canyon Trust has worked tirelessly to protect the wild heart of the West. (Grand Canyon Trust Website)

Both the Bears Ears and Grand Staircase-Escalante monuments have been a source of political turmoil after Republicans blasted their establishment under Presidents Barack Obama and Bill Clinton as an overreach by the federal government. Utah lawmakers, including Senators Orrin Hatch and Mike Lee, applauded President Donald Trump for his decision to reduce the size of both monuments, with Lee saying he was "grateful" that the president was "sympathetic to the fact that we've been mistreated."

The Secret

The unknown dirty little secret is that as part of these designations, which even most supporters do not know or realize, the real property (and other assets like mineral rights) is transferred to the ownership of the United States Government and as such these rights automatically become the collateral that secures all of the debts belonging to the United States of America. Said ownership can be used to restrain or negotiate other transactions like Uranium One with the Russians.- AND WHAT IS LOCATED WITHIN THE GRAND STAIRCASE MONUMENT? One of the world's largest and most potent uranium deposits!

Hummm? Who set this into play? Well, look at that, it was none other than William Jefferson Clinton clear back in 1996. the same Bill Clinton, with his co-conspirator spouse Hillary, aided and supported by numerous individuals on both side of the political aisle, who have financially benefited from the Clinton Foundation, as they sold out America and its interest to our enemies...

Other elected official in Utah know what the monument fight is all about (ownership rights - not just control,) but they do not have the courage to let the people know because it would expose the rotten truth about our elected officials. - And None would dare call it a conspiracy!

Final Note

There is one simple rule to remember when it comes to Mortgage Fraud, Public or Corporate Corruption, or frankly any form of White Collar Crime, if you want to know who's behind it? Follow the Money! Now take a look at whose names keep coming up in the middle of all of these controversies and corruption. It is pretty telling. ***Where there is smoke, there is fire!***

May we remember Alexander Fraser Tytler's warning, *"A democracy cannot exist as a permanent form of government. It can only exist until the voters discover that they can vote themselves largesse from the public treasury. From that moment on, the majority always votes for the candidates promising the most benefits from the public treasury with the result that a democracy always collapses over loose fiscal policy, always followed by a dictatorship. The average age of the world's greatest civilizations has been 200 years. These nations have progressed through this sequence: From bondage to spiritual faith; From spiritual faith to great courage; From courage to liberty; From liberty to abundance; From abundance to selfishness; From selfishness to apathy; From apathy to dependence; From dependence back into bondage."*

Sadly, we here in America have returned to the crossroad where we were over 240 years ago under the tyrannical domination of a Kingship; only now (we) the U.S. Government is the oppressor. The question is, which direction will America go? One road leads to a nation of people dependent on the government for every aspect of their lives, and servants to the whims of the oppressor. The other path leads to renewed liberties and freedom where "we, the people," have the choice to become whatever we choose to be.

I hope for America, and all of us, that we make the wise choice.

ABOUT THE AUTHOR

Thomas H. (Tom) Fairbanks has been involved in real estate, business, and economic development for the last 40+ years; specializing in incubation facilitation, which is an economic lifeline of business support, resources, and services that accelerate the growth and success of startup and entrepreneurial enterprises.

A man with extensive experience in the integration of business, real estate investments and personal development. His extensive entrepreneurial career began with his first sole entrepreneurial effort at the age of 22. He is a continual student in human behavior and participated in the development of a personal and professional development-training program used to educate clients and incubated companies.

He is a firm believer in the power of association, and his extensive hands-on education has helped him to develop and author the concepts of SupplyLine Economics©, and Collaborative Business Systems©. Having witnessed firsthand the abuses of ethical violations in business, Tom became an active proponent of fair play and community advocacy and his efforts led to the formulating of the "Principles of Good Business©" which he believes is the core foundation of healthy business and community development.

His wife, Shauna, presented Tom with a certificate of achievement for Christmas many years ago acknowledging that he was successfully completing an Advanced Ongoing Course in the Field of Life. This was the impetus to the creation of the School of Hard Knocks.

Thomas H. Fairbanks

References

Leonard Pitts Jr., *The Miami Herald Opinion Column* dated September 12, 2001. Quote on Page 1-2.

W. Cleon Skousen, *"The Five Thousand Year Leap"* 1981. Quotes on Pages 4-7.

Robert B. Stinnett, *"Day of Deceit: The Truth about FDR and Pearl Harbor"* 2000. Full Quote Pages 9-16 obtained from: www.lewrockwell.com/2016/12/no_author/pearl-harbor-fake-news-story/ http://www.washingtonsblog.com/2016/12/pearl-harbor-facts-proof.html

Old Testament (KJV,) - *1 Samuel Chapter 8* Quotes on Page 19.

Robert K. Greenleaf, "The Servant as Leader" 1970, and ""The Institution as Servant" 1972. References and Quotes on Pages 23-25.

Dr George Kaufman, *"Shortened version of a paper presented at the International Conference on Bad Enterprise Debts in Central and Eastern Europe"* in Budapest, Hungary on June 6-8, 1994. At: https://fee.org/articles/the-us-banking-debacle-of-the-1980s-a-lesson-in-government-mismanagement/, Full Quote on Pages 35-45.

Valerie Richardson, The Washington Times, *"AG Sessions orders examination of Bundy case after mistrial over prosecution bungling -Government failed to turn over evidence,"* December 21, 2017. Full Quote on Pages 69-72.

Kevin Sullivan and Juliet Eilperin, The Washington Post, *"In the Nevada desert, Bundy family warns of another standoff,"* November 1, 2016. Full Quote on Pages 72-77.

Marcus Stern, Reuters Business News, *"U.S. Senator Reid, son combine for China firm's desert plant,"* August 30, 2012. Quote on pages 77-78.

Katie Bo Williams, The Hill, *"WikiLeaks releases alleged Podesta emails,"* October 7, 2016. Quote on Page 78.

Jo Becker and Mike McIntire, The New York Times, *"Cash Flowed to Clinton Foundation Amid Russian Uranium Deal,"* APRIL 23, 2015. Full Quote on Pages 78-92.

Made in the USA
San Bernardino, CA
19 September 2018